442577

EDITOR
MAX FRASER

REVIEWER
ELLEN HIMELFARB

RESTAURANT EDITOR
GEMMA BELL

PICTURE RESEARCHER
LIZ BOYD

DESIGN
RICHARD ARDAGH STUDIO

COVER DESIGN
HANNAH WALDRON

PUBLISHER
MAX FRASER

CONTRIBUTORS
MICHAEL ANASTASSIADES
AMY BICKNELL
JAMES BROWN
SAM & SAM CLARKE
YVONNE COURTNEY
PETER DORE-SMITH
LIZZIE EVANS
JO FROUDE
SIOBHAN GILLESPIE
SAM JACOB
MATS KLINGBERG
PETER LAYTON
ALISON LLOYD
SARA NORRMAN
LULU ROPER-CALDBECK
NEIL SAUNDERS
ANNE SOWARD
STEPHEN WEBSTER
MARK WEEKS

It is with extraordinary pride that I welcome you to the 2014-2015 edition of *London* ... only publication dedicated excl... ...estinations. Pride be... ...s to the third totally ... ...print is experiencing ... ...utward looking a... ...d marvel at its ... ...obal stage. As ... ...nt article, 'London is the des... ...orld.'

Having lived in London for over 30 years, I have come to understand that this city will certainly provide a lifetime of learning and discovery. This vast cosmopolitan capital is layered with dynamic history, illustrating at every turn the enormous cultural role it has played in the world until now and that it continues to play with all the gusto and determination of its people. Indeed, it's the people of the city that enrich its material magnificence, injecting a highly charged pulse into the multicultural neighbourhoods of the capital.

Design's role is present everywhere, spanning the mundane to the spectacular. It is the latter that we champion in this guide, offering you a snapshot of the burgeoning design scene that you can access today. My team and I have tirelessly scoured the city, hunting out the best design shops, galleries, museums, bookshops and eateries for you to enjoy.

To help you navigate this plethora of places, we've divided the city into design-heavy neighbourhoods and marked each featured destination on maps. My advice is to tackle one area at a time by foot, immersing yourself in the locality and taking in the street scenes that unfold at every turn.

And while you're travelling to these places, have a read of the essays and discussions that pepper the pages of this guide. In this edition, we've examined the state of retail during a period when shops are undoubtedly struggling with a weak economy, tapered footfall, high rents and the great might of internet shopping. What's the future trajectory of bricks-and-mortar shops, of the very kind we support in *London Design Guide*?

Well, I have full faith that London's ability to continually question and reinvent itself will propel its armies of complacency-busting entrepreneurs to greater things. I invite you to take part in this journey of perpetual discovery and may design be your guide.

We welcome feedback and
recommendations:
info@londondesignguide.com

PUBLISHED BY SPOTLIGHT PRESS

Max Fraser

BERNHARDT | design

GEN REF
745
LON

Contents

GUIDELINES AND CRITERIA

The definition of 'design' in this guide refers to three-dimensional objects in the broadest sense, and furniture, lighting, ceramics, glass, textiles and tableware more specifically, as well as some graphic art and contemporary prints. The guide reviews businesses open to the public, so it doesn't include references to studios, or interior and architecture practices.

We have chosen to exclude the following: shops devoted to 'permanents', such as bathroom and kitchen appliances, tiles, flooring, light fixtures, etc; office-furniture showrooms; shops with stock comprising more than 50 per cent clothing; businesses with an 'appointment only' opening policy; businesses that are utterly unbearable to deal with (you know who you are). In very few cases, there are exceptions to this criteria.

London's boundary is defined by the M25 orbital motorway. No neighbourhood was predetermined – all were defined after we had researched, visited and approved every place. We defined each area by the high concentration of design activity within it, afterwards adding recommendations for the *Eat & drink* sections concluding each chapter. The maps that open each chapter are illustrative and include streets that are relevant to the entries in the guide. We recommend carrying a comprehensive street map for a greater overview.

Most importantly, no person or business has paid to be included in the editorial portions of this guide, nor can any exert pressure on us to tailor the reviews. Research visits were anonymous and unannounced to ensure a genuine customer experience. Clothes worn were casual with no outward display of wealth.

Now that's clear, please enjoy!

Cleverly
put
together.

ES 01
Extension Socket designed by Georges Moanack
shop.punktgroup.com

US version of the ES 01 used for illustrative purposes only,
other country versions also available.

Function. Design. Simplicity.

Punkt.

Notting Hill
&
Ladbroke Grove

p.035

Marylebone

p.049

Soho
&
Fitzrovia

p.077

Mayfair

p.065

Chelsea,
Knightsbridge
&
Brompton

p.009

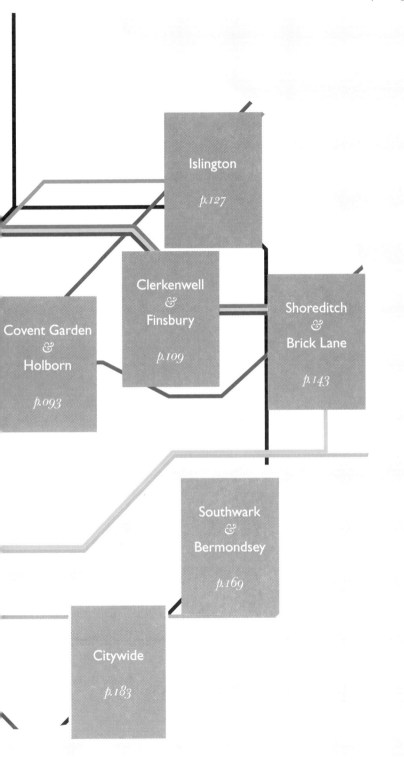

Islington

p.127

Clerkenwell
&
Finsbury

p.109

Covent Garden
&
Holborn

p.093

Shoreditch
&
Brick Lane

p.143

Southwark
&
Bermondsey

p.169

Citywide

p.183

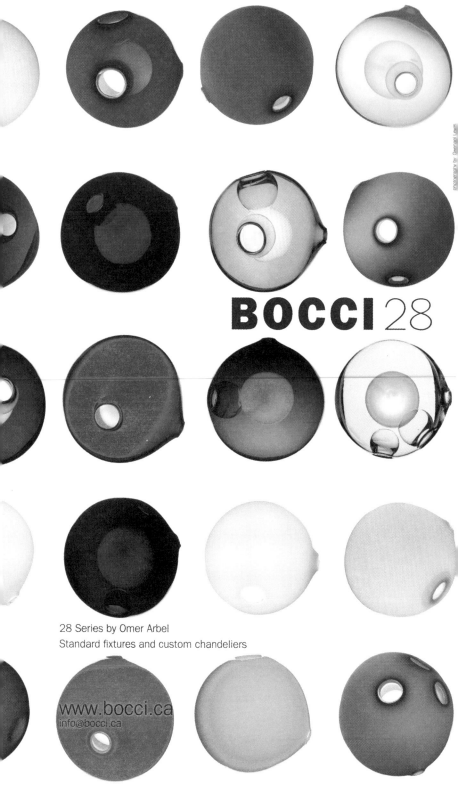

BOCCI 28

28 Series by Omer Arbel
Standard fixtures and custom chandeliers

Chelsea, Knightsbridge & Brompton

S.W.1.
SW3
SW7

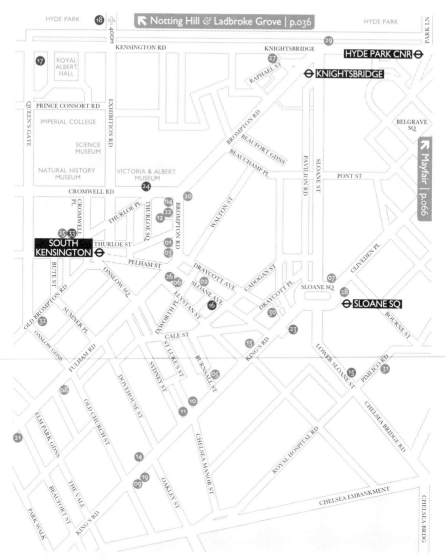

↖ Notting Hill & Ladbroke Grove | p.036

↗ Mayfair | p.066

- ● *Design galleries & institutions*
- ● *Design shops & C20th vintage*
- ● *Design bookshops*

- ● *Eat & drink (pp.026-027)*

01 B&B ITALIA	13 MUJI *p.091*
02 BISAZZA	14 POLIFORM
03 BOFFI	15 POTTERTON BOOKS
04 CASSINA	16 RABIH HAGE
05 CHRISTOPHER FARR	17 ROYAL COLLEGE OF ART
06 THE CONRAN SHOP	18 SERPENTINE GALLERY
07 DAVID MELLOR	19 SIGMAR
08 DE PARMA	20 SKANDIUM
09 DESIGNER'S GUILD	21 SOLID ID
10 HABITAT *p.085*	22 SQUINT
11 HEAL'S *p.085*	23 TASCHEN
12 MINT	24 VICTORIA AND ALBERT MUSEUM

Street*wise*

When did you move to this street?
September 2006.

What originally attracted you to it?
With the best fishmonger in London round the corner (Chelsea Fishmonger) and Jago Butchers next door, we felt that this spot would be ideal for us. Chelsea Green retains a real sense of community, both between businesses and local customers who actively support the neighbourhood shops. The area was missing a decent wine merchant and with a customer base already in this part of London, it made sense to make this move. What is more, HH&C started life in Kensington Church Street, so by returning to the Royal Borough we've had several customers returning who bought wine from us in the 1980s.

How has the surrounding area changed since you've been here?
The area has lost one or two businesses and it has been sad to see shops lie empty. However, in the last few years the shopping thoroughfare has improved and the business community has become more tightly knit. The arrival of Andreas's fruit and vegetable store just over a year ago, and the addition of a café to Finns gourmet food shop, have given shoppers an extra incentive to visit the area.

What does the street offer the community that is unique?
Elystan Street offers a range of independent shops and services, many of which have long histories of being in the area. The sense of community and attention to high quality personal service are second to none. With Chelsea Green 10 seconds away, we are unique as a one-stop shop. You can buy all your fresh produce and wine locally, and sit down to an al fresco lunch while getting your dry cleaning and shoe repairs done.

Tell us about some of your neighbouring hotspots.
For excellent quality produce, the Chelsea Fishmonger and Andreas cannot be beaten. Finns of Chelsea Green is a superb delicatessen and Real Hair is a top hairdressing salon. Many of these are key to why we are here.

What do you think is missing from the street?
The one thing that Elystan Street and Chelsea Green lacks is a good cheese shop. We would love to see an independent cheese shop take residence here – it would be well received and supported.

Siobhán Gillespie
Haynes Hanson & Clark

7 ELYSTAN STREET SW3 3NT
020 7584 7927 HHANDC.CO.UK

ELYSTAN STREET

01 B&B ITALIA

- 250 BROMPTON ROAD SW3 2AS
- 020 7591 8111
- BEBITALIA.IT
- MON-SAT 10-6, SUN 12-5
- SOUTH KENSINGTON

The cavernous B&B flagship is not only a store, it's an experience. Behind a two-storey glass frontage, the former car showroom, converted by venerated architect John Pawson and designed by Antonio Citterio, swoops and soars deep into Brompton Cross – 120 metres deep. Indeed, you could drive a car through it.

A giant of Italian modernism, B&B, at nearly 50, is one certainty in a very uncertain Italy. It produces staples that are elegantly refined yet unshowy, ample yet unimposing, vibrant yet subtly so. You can sniff at the top-end prices, but, really, when amortised over a lifetime – for a B&B piece has the integrity to last at least that long – they'll likely match those half-dozen IKEA sofas you'll surely wear through.

Spend a half hour wandering through the tantalising room sets, past the giant carved-wood screens that separate them. Compare Citterio's classic couches with the more approachable Maxalto collections (comparable design without the big name attached), then settle, as I did, into a Jeffrey Bernett rocking chaise longue. Nobody will rush to offer you assistance, giving you time to contemplate its place within your home.

02 BISAZZA

60 SLOANE AVENUE SW3 3DD

020 7584 8837

BISAZZA.COM

MON–SAT 10–6

SOUTH KENSINGTON

The first thing you might notice about Bisazza's Chelsea headquarters is the enormous round Marcel Wanders-designed tub. Or Wanders' pebble-shaped mosaic coffee tables in the window. Or the shower affixed to the ceiling amid a spray of crystals, the only hint that it's not a chandelier offered by the two red taps emerging from the wall. What I noticed was the scent, a florid peachy bouquet that made me want to settle in for a long soak.

The affable assistant who showed me around what might be the largest in-store toilet in London, plastered wall-to-wall in a vivid floral mosaic, couldn't even detect the smell, having spent so much time in these parts she'd been desensitised. But she seemed to so enjoy her job, the fragrant atmosphere had obviously sunk in.

A tour through the premises is exceptionally pleasurable. Down a dramatic swooping staircase, the lower level is another delight, floors coated in a mosaic that feels exhilarating to walk on, even in thick-soled boots. Of course, the company has always been about drama, using their iridescent mosaics to Renaissance-grade effect. The artful scenes are a perfect complement to the new Wanders and Jaime Hayon bathroom lines, available here. If you have a space like this Sloane Avenue jewel, all the better.

03 BOFFI CHELSEA
- 254 BROMPTON ROAD SW3 2AS
- 020 7590 8910
- BOFFIUK.COM
- MON-SAT 10-6
- SOUTH KENSINGTON

The yin to B&B Italia's yang next door, the Boffi showroom is reached by a dim, moody corridor past a pair of receptionists seated like guardians of the gates. It should be intimidating, but it's not. Persevere along that hallway and enter the Boffi world, all charcoal walls and architectural furnishings that reveal nothing of their function but are, in actuality, highly functional kitchens and baths. Rather than mere fodder for BBC magazines, however, these kitchens and baths occupy an echelon of their own.

Like its neighbour B&B, the Boffi showroom goes on for miles but is an entirely different experience: intense, dramatic and accessorised not with dividing screens but walls of bamboo. These soften the severe lines of the product and give the rooms more of a lounge feel, enhanced by some warmer details like wooden dining bars, textured tiling and seagrass walls. A Boffi space is a space to be lived in, no matter what the ultimate purpose – which is why we feature them here.

04 CASSINA
- 242 BROMPTON ROAD SW3 2BB
- 020 7584 0000
- CASSINA.COM
- MON-WED, FRI-SAT 10-6.30, THU 10-7, SUN 12-6
- SOUTH KENSINGTON

The locals might have sensed that not all would be lost with the departure of their beloved Few and Far, the whimsical Priscilla Carluccio boutique. They might have also sensed its replacement would be Italian, seeing as the next block is the adopted home of B&B Italia and Boffi, bringing an army of wildly gesticulating shop assistants to the neighbourhood. Indeed, last year Brompton Cross welcomed Cassina, in a strategically lit showroom redesigned with steely aplomb by Piero Lissoni.

At nearly 90 years old, the Cassina brand has had its share of contributors, and this space reflects that. In one corner you might find a pair of ladder-back *Hill House* chairs by Charles Rennie Mackintosh (an unlikely collaborator among the Corbusiers and Perriands) enhanced by a vertical arrangement of gilt mirrors. And in another a newly designed Patrick Norguet *P22* wing chair (more sumptuous than it sounds) by a *Cicognino* side table by Franco Albini. In yet another corner you might spot a team of shop managers doing business on a Philippe Starck *My World* sofa. They might not jump up to greet you, but they'll look so comfortable, they couldn't offer a better advertisement for the product.

When rugs started becoming a medium for artists and designers, the development suited Christopher Farr just fine. The Slade-trained painter established himself in the 1980s before he started dealing in floor coverings and ultimately launching an eponymous business, using his eye for colour and pattern to transform the floor into the fifth wall.

A precursor to the more commercial Rug Company, Farr was a pioneer in commissioning big-name creatives to turn their attentions downward. He has worked with the likes of Andrée Putman, Kate Blee and Romeo Gigli on limited-edition designs, later adding fabrics to his catalogue. And earlier this year he celebrated his 25th anniversary in the business with a show of collectible rugs at Somerset House, featuring works by a spectrum of contributors including Josef Albers and Lara Bohinc.

True to his origins, Farr's showroom off the King's Road is more like an atelier, encompassing his studio, stockroom and collection of samples in the same barn-like space. You may feel slightly self-conscious, stepping over stacks of rugs to access your preferred colourway, but the benefit is that the staff are all there to hand, eager to talk you through the customisation process.

05 CHRISTOPHER FARR
6 BURNSALL STREET SW3 3ST
020 7349 0888
CHRISTOPHERFARR.COM
MON-FRI 10-6
SLOANE SQUARE

The Conran Shop has lived longer than most Britons and doesn't seem anywhere near retirement. This Chelsea flagship is the reason. Just when you think you might be tiring of the whole Conran ethos, the space is transformed with a new attitude and lease of life, thanks in part to Jasper Conran's recent appointment as creative director. His influence has brought about a decluttering, a fresh lick of white paint and a look that is decidedly more fun and continental.

The main floor is like a vast West End stage, with various levels supporting spic-and-span room sets, overwhelmingly neutral in tone (even the books on the shelves are white – evidently a trend these days) with splashes of colour in throw cushions and serving pieces. Conran's own-designed living and dining furniture gets good play but also features well alongside favourites by Bertoia and Benchmark.

Despite the heritage stock, this is a store you won't feel sheepish about entering with the entire family. At any one moment, there are dozens – dozens! – of assistants on the floor, each one super-charged and task oriented, so hyper kids feel right at home. Plus, there's a Moroccan-themed bazaar on the lower level heaped with toys and textiles, along with a play area proper.

06 THE CONRAN SHOP CHELSEA
MICHELIN HOUSE, 81 FULHAM ROAD SW3 6RD
020 7589 7401
CONRANSHOP.CO.UK
MON-FRI 10-6, WED-THU 10-7, SA 10-6:30, SU 12-6
SOUTH KENSINGTON

Sloane Square isn't the first place you'd expect to find a Sheffield-born family business, but David Mellor has the appropriate amount of gleam. The tableware retailer, a fixture here since Woodstock, stocks the full range of Mellor's finely designed, hand-crafted cutlery – the staple of many a Sloaney dinner party, and pretty much every other dignified event in the country. The stainless steel and silverware is presented, standing to attention, along one wall, while the other, in the cosy wedge of a space, displays serving pieces by Mellor and a stable of brands and designers, among them iittala and Sarah Petherick, who makes a range of bowls and spoons from Vietnamese water buffalo horn.

This is not it, though. Mellor, now run by Mellor's son Corin, has a lower level that trumps the ground-floor space in size and scope. This is where you'll find small appliances, pottery, gardening tools, and even homemade jams. These pieces change with advancements in technology and design, but for the most part the shop remains now as it always has been, a refuge of quality and comfort.

Fulham Road is a sea of heavy upholsteries and curtain tassels until you reach De Parma, suitably urbane for the neighbourhood, yet far more cool. De Parma's collectible midcentury design, also found online at 1stdibs.com, skews older than a lot of the modernism so long in vogue in the eastern reaches of the city. Gary De Sparham's curated collection focuses on the 1940s and '50s, predating the Danish invasion and appearing more elegant – Hollywood by way of Italy.

De Sparham has an obvious fascination with the Italian heavies of the era: there is always something in store representing Ico Parisi, Gio Ponti or Piero Fornasetti – a pair of Ponti lamps for Christofle, a Fornasetti cabinet, or perhaps a serpentine chaise longue by Parisi. Added excitement comes in through accessories like kinetic floor lamps by Stilnovo and Manuel Marín's Calder-esque mobiles.

Downstairs I found a 1960s Carrera marble coffee table, produced by Skipper, with a toothy pattern cut into each side so the length could expand along the notches. It's hard to explain here – you'll have to ask the savvy manager to show you in person.

Some way into her decades-long career Tricia Guild realised man (or, more likely, woman) could not live on sumptuous textiles alone, no matter how juicy the colours. This showroom is the product of Guild's successful formula of unusual midcentury design, eccentric artwork and one-off accessories, all adhering to the highly saturated palette continuously refreshed by the designer. The formula works, not least because it takes some of the pressure off the textiles and allows them to be showcased imaginatively on soft furnishings by Fritz Hansen and Moroso.

This is a deep, multi-level space but never feels that way, surprising as it is at every dip and bend. Vitrines of jewellery, not to mention a gift-wrapping station that could transform a tech-junkie into a scribe, jive with the feminine spirit. But more macho companions will appreciate the garden stuffed with painted loungers and the Chesterfield sofas tufted with men's tailoring. Or they could just settle into one and wait.

09 DESIGNERS GUILD
267 & 277 KING'S ROAD SW3 5EN
020 7351 5775
DESIGNERSGUILD.COM
MON-SAT 10-6, SUN 12-5
SLOANE SQUARE/SOUTH KENSINGTON

Lina Kanafani is the sage on the mountain of design retailers, blessed with a special sense for what will catch the fancy of the discerning independent-design enthusiast. Her shop may have relocated to the heart of London's European establishment, but her stock has nothing in common with the continental brands – with anybody for that matter. Rather it stocks incomparable works of functional art, much of it from young unknowns, that surely must have been a thrill to curate.

What first catches your eye are the vessels, potted pieces that meld ancient techniques with contemporary glazes and finishes, and the unusual wood and blown-glass vessel-shaped artworks by London-based Pia Wüstenberg – some of it remarkably affordable. Then it's the rich collection of armchairs: immaculately upholstered vintage wingbacks and Chesterfield-style club chairs set in foundations of natural birchbark. Of course, there are others who could track down chandeliers draped in ball chains or sculpted with copper tubes, but Kanafani layers them with the expertise of a Hollywood set designer. Undoubtedly, she has a great eye for distinct design, so it is hardly surprising that she operates an interior-design consultation from the premises for those who want to buy wholeheartedly into her vision.

12 MINT
2 NORTH TERRACE SW3 2BA
020 7225 2228
MINTSHOP.CO.UK
MON-SAT 10:30-6:30, THU 10:30-7:30
SOUTH KENSINGTON

(14) POLIFORM

- 278 KING'S ROAD SW3 5AW
- 020 7368 7600
- POLIFORMUK.COM
- MON–SAT 10–6
- SLOANE SQUARE

It seems fitting that Poliform has come to roost in the consumer heartland King's Road rather than the tradesman-preferred Brompton Cross; it seems a bit samey, just that bit more sterile than its Italian peers, with spare, geometric tables and sectionals, and wardrobe systems that prop themselves with three crisp white shirts. Still, it's keeping up with the Joneses, albeit the wealthy ones; 40 years in business, and more than a decade in its Paolo Piva-designed London flagship, and it shows no signs of flailing.

There are highlights, of course: the ranges from Jean-Marie Massaud, including the iconic *Ventura Lounge*, shown in electric blue; and Paola Navone's irresistible *Bug* armchair. If you're looking for a kitchen, the high spec Varenna kitchens are fitted with slick Gaggenau appliances. To help soften the hard-lined Italian look, check out the sumptuous rugs at Stepevi's flagship right next door.

(15) POTTERTON BOOKS

- 93 LOWER SLOANE STREET SW1W 8DA
- 020 7730 4235
- POTTERTONBOOKSLONDON.COM
- MON–SAT 10–6, SUN 11–5
- SLOANE SQUARE

It's a rather depressing reality that, in our high-street world, a bookstore has to ask you to come in and feel free to browse – once upon a time, it was an unspoken rule. Nevertheless, that is Potterton's request, and you should take them up on it.

You might balk: Potterton is a veritable cabinet and where you might physically wander through other bookshops, here you can't do much more than shuffle to the opposite stacks. The content is worth a go, though, because the speciality here is 'inspiration' – anything that might inspire you to creativity between four wonky walls. Printing, fashion, photography, crafts, garden design, architecture… it's all here, sometimes in rare form, often signed by local authors such as Nicky Haslam, whose design consultancy is located over the road. Unbelievable as it may seem, the diminutive walls also serve as a backdrop for folk art and graphic design.

 RABIH HAGE

- 69-71 SLOANE AVENUE SW3 3DH
- 020 7823 8288
- RABIH-HAGE.COM
- MON-SAT 10-6
- SOUTH KENSINGTON

Don't make the mistake of looking for price tags on Rabih Hage's artful design; this Sloane Avenue space is a gallery first, a platform for acclaimed designers like Gaetano Pesce, Piet Hein Eek and mechatronics supremo Moritz Waldemeyer, as well as Hage himself, naturally. For your own Hage piece you'll have to hire the man himself, though, who works from the adjacent design studio, sometimes poking out his head to see who's interested.

One of the first 'design artists', whose cleverly calculated collectible furnishings have appeared in exhibitions across Europe, Hage possesses a feeling for unusual materials and a personality for translating them into a comfortably liveable thing. His *Leftover Collection* for Corian, exhibited at Salone in Milan in 2012, flaunted the versatility of the product but also of his own practice of using workaday materials (even offcuts thereof) to create surreal beauty. If you don't make it to Chelsea, visit the website of DeTnk, his online think thank and video gallery.

ROYAL COLLEGE OF ART

KENSINGTON GORE SW7 2EU

020 7590 4444

RCA.AC.UK

[OPEN TO THE PUBLIC DURING SELECT PERIODS]

HIGH STREET KENSINGTON/SOUTH KENSINGTON

Sometimes you have to go back to move forward. Which is to say, it can't hurt to check out what the kids are doing these days for inspiration to greater things. The RCA's creative MA curriculum is one of the world's most prestigious; alumni include names as disparate as David Adjaye, David Hockney, Alison Jackson, Philip Treacy and Idris Khan. The current student body is unknown, for now, but one day you'll be able to boast that you purchased one of their creatively-charged designs 'back when' at the annual graduate Summer Show, an event that attracts gallerists and trendhunters to the school each June.

Or you could attend the May fashion shows and anticipate the trends you'll see in TopShop next year. Both are open to the public, along with a programme of free lectures and exhibitions held at the school galleries and staggered throughout the year.

The college is advantageously located near the V&A (p.025) and Natural History Museum (more inspiration), and just crossing the threshold into the reception hall can heighten your senses.

18 SERPENTINE GALLERY

KENSINGTON GARDENS W2 3XA

020 7402 6075

SERPENTINEGALLERY.ORG

DAILY 10-6

KNIGHTSBRIDGE/SOUTH KENSINGTON/LANCASTER GT.

London's weather being what it is, a warm, cultural escape at the centre of Hyde Park can only be a good thing. But the Serpentine is much more than its classical structure would suggest. The interior is incongruously modern, right up to the windowed cupola and the expertly curated indie bookshop of art and architecture titles run by Koenig (p.100). And the artists invited by directors Hans-Ulrich Obrist and Julia Peyton-Jones are esteemed ground-breakers, from Thomas Demand and Bridget Riley to Yoko Ono and Rosemarie Trockel, whose textile-based works recently included several experiments in dreamlike upholstered seating.

The gallery dabbles in design-art, recently collaborating with Konstantin Grcic on an exhibition of high-impact everyday design. But it has become better known for its celebration of contemporary architecture. Its highly anticipated annual summer pavilions by legends like Jean Nouvel and Herzog & de Meuron (collaborating with Ai Weiwei) express a fascination for the medium that the gallery proper cannot.

Recently, the gallery expanded into a second space across the eponymous river: the 900-square-metre Serpentine Sackler Gallery. The renovation and development of a 200-year-old Palladian building, with a new café annex, was realised by Zaha Hadid Architects, and hosts emerging talents in the fields of architecture, design, film, fashion, art, music and technology.

19 SIGMAR

- 263 KING'S ROAD SW3 5EL
- 020 7751 5801
- SIGMARLONDON.COM
- MON–SAT 10-6, SUN 12-5
- SLOANE SQUARE/SOUTH KENSINGTON

It's not big; it's a big deal, though. On the King's Road, where the tone leans toward pomp and circumstance, Sigmar offers thoughtful, streamlined, enchanting treasures from northern Europe's golden years (1940s to '60s, mostly) and a few treats from today. Run by Ebba Thott and Nina Hertig, interiors experts with extraordinary enthusiasm, it packs more into the first square metre than many shops carry across the floor.

On my last visit, I was hardly past the door before Hertig rushed over to enlighten me on a pair of curious brass shelves (by the Austrian brass-master Carl Auböck; £2,400 for the set) and an extraordinary series of wall-mounted Pierre Forsell candlesticks. Metallics are a refined accent throughout the space. Some of Sigmar's only contemporary wares are from local darling Michael Anastassiades (p.195), whose latest lighting collection in gold, chrome and patinated brass is a cut above; I particularly enjoyed his gold *Beauty Mirror* (£1,500), so called because of the glow it gives your skin no matter what your complexion. Quality prevails across everything in Sigmar, ideal for those hunting for design that lasts.

20 SKANDIUM

- 245–249 BROMPTON ROAD SW3 2EP
- 020 7584 2066
- SKANDIUM.COM
- MON–SAT 10-6:30, THU 10-7, SUN 11-5
- SOUTH KENSINGTON

Within this sizeable corner space in Brompton, Skandium customers can enjoy browsing a carefully curated display of Scandinavian classics, new innovations and a smattering of kitsch, together with complementary pieces from other European brands. The ground floor houses a strong collection of delicate glassware and elegant ceramics by iittala, Orrefors and Marimekko, amid other beautiful and functional additions for the home. You'd do well to pick up a gift here, with prices suiting a range of budgets.

Owners Magnus Englund, Chrystina Schmidt and Christopher Seidenfaden import only what they love – continually introducing new offerings that distinguish them from the now ubiquitous Scandi purveyors found elsewhere. The unifying theme is 'design to last'. I was reminded of as much when I headed to the basement to hunt down a match for a wall hook I'd purchased a decade earlier. After demonstrating a glossy red stepladder by Design House Stockholm, a friendly and helpful assistant asked if I was still using it and seemed thrilled to hear that I was. "Good design will stand the test of time," he reminded me. No matter that he couldn't find what I was looking for. His words eased the sting.

If it lights up or used to breathe, chances are it'll make it onto the floor at Solid ID, a boutique that stocks old fairground signs and sculptural taxidermy like the props department of a fringe theatre. Should that deter you, consider the reputable Dutch duo behind it, Eelke Jan Bles and Robert Weems, also run Solid Floor, the wood-flooring experts that furnish London institutions like Ottolenghi and McQueens florist, and projects by every starchitect from David Chipperfield to Zaha Hadid.

The MO in store is: nothing that doesn't make a statement. Indeed, the backstory is as integral to the product as the product itself, the drama often favoured over practicality (correct me, though, if a pair of carved-wood angel wings were just the thing you were looking for to dangle over your lounge). That said, the adversely impractical finds are reworked and repurposed, and displayed with new designs, like jewellery by Jessica de Lotz and hand-painted cushions by Fairlyte. The mix is constantly refreshed, the distressed furniture, oversized glassware and vintage lighting shuffled around the company's trademark parquet.

㉑ SOLID ID

🏠 273 FULHAM ROAD SW10 9PZ
📞 020 7351 3045
🖊 SOLIDID.CO.UK
🕐 MON-FRI 10:30-6, SAT 10:30-5
⊖ GLOUCESTER ROAD/SOUTH KENSINGTON

While the presence on Shoreditch High Street is a repository for designs en route to the customer, this quaint outbuilding off Brompton Road is considered Squint HQ. Reached past a black-painted entrance way, the showroom takes the popular patchwork motif to the max, and perhaps overboard, to the point where you can't see much else but squares of Skittles-hued velvet.

You should persevere, though; there are alternatives in the mix, if equally colourful. Hand-embroidered Thai cushions, for instance, are a riot. Strangely incongruous but just as delightful are table lamps designed by John Mayle from glass reclaimed from defunct schools. Then, down an industrial metal staircase, is an unfinished space with legions of chandeliers – styled with traditional French flourishes yet wrapped in jewel-toned velvet. A controversial cup of tea, perhaps, but a consistent vision.

㉒ SQUINT

🏠 1 NORTH TERRACE SW3 2BA
📞 020 7589 6839
🖊 SQUINTLIMITED.COM
🕐 MON-SAT 10-6, THU 10-7, SUN 12-5
⊖ SOUTH KENSINGTON

 23 TASCHEN

- 12 DUKE OF YORK SQUARE SW3 4LY
- 020 7881 0795
- TASCHEN.COM
- MON-TUE, THU-FRI 10-6, WED, SAT 10-7, SUN 12-6
- SLOANE SQUARE

Unless you're Chanel or Vuitton, it's nigh on impossible to pull off the monobrand shop, so we'll put Taschen in the category of high-design bookstore, capable of doing monobrand with flair. The brand, founded by the German patriarch Benedikt, has done well by hiring Philippe Starck to outfit its Chelsea store, two snug spaces stacked one upon the other, building a series of immense storage islands down the middle to serve as browsing stations. Nobody's hiding the imprint's exhibitionist tendencies here: titles like *Bondage* by Nobuyoshi Araki and *The Big Book of Pussy* are laid bare on the plinths, alongside the new Sebastião Salgado and the wonderful *36 Hours: 125 Weekends in Europe*. Taschen's travel series is stacked in back.

If these don't grab you, descend to the store's depths, organised like an East End gallery complete with framed vintage prints, an antique Esther scroll, a 10-kilo LaChapelle monograph and the odd inflatable dolphin. Nobody can blame them for poor merchandising. Or for their choice of real estate: say what you will about the plain-vanilla Duke of York Square – it has never looked this good.

2.4 VICTORIA AND ALBERT MUSEUM

- CROMWELL ROAD SW7 2RL
- 020 7942 2000
- VAM.AC.UK
- DAILY 10-5:45, FRI 10-10
- SOUTH KENSINGTON

You know contemporary furniture design has arrived when the world's most distinguished design museum is paying homage. In 2012, the Italian Renaissance-style palace enjoyed an overhaul of its upper floor, a reimagined ceramics gallery and the new Dr Susan Weber Furniture Gallery, occupying a series of brilliantly lit colonnades. Contents date back to the 15th century, but the hype surrounding the rich cache of modernists from Frank Lloyd Wright and Eileen Gray to Ron Arad.

The V&A is committed to documenting contemporary design and architecture; it hosted a Thomas Heatherwick retrospective in 2012, along with a five-month exhibition covering innovative British design from 1948. But its collection spans 2,000 years of design on all continents. The building is a suitable venue. Its regal spaces are ample enough that even the most monolithic marbles – and attendant mobs – can breathe. Some rooms are constructed almost entirely of architectural relics.

The building is Louvre-esque in scope, its wings split and fractured so it can seem an eternity to travel between floors. There's enough on the ground floor, however, to make a brief visit worthwhile. Temporary exhibitions are centrally located, along with the Fashion and Sculpture galleries, and legions of Asian tapestries. Recharge in the café or rest your legs in the John Madejski Garden, a blessed retreat in summer.

25 *Mediterranean lunch*

Informal basement restaurant and bar that manages
to be light and airy. White tiles, brass fittings, stunning
blue leather stalls, bentwood chairs, big silver bowls of
Sicilian lemons arranged on the bar. Mediterranean
menu that is well executed and unfussy.

APERO [PICTURED] 2 HARRINGTON ROAD SW7 3ER
020 7591 4410 | APERORESTAURANTANDBAR.COM

26 *Conran institution*

Elegant dining room serving classic French dishes
with British influence. Original setting in the iconic
Michelin House with stunning stained-glass windows
and Art Deco furniture. Oyster bar perfect pitstop
for a seafood platter and glass of Champagne.

BIBENDUM MICHELIN HOUSE, 81 FULHAM ROAD SW3 6RD
020 7581 5817 | BIBENDUM.CO.UK

27 *Dinner for under £20*

Old-school French bistro hidden down a
Knightsbridge alley, could be in Paris. Red and
white tablecloths and dark wood throughout. Bargain
set menus or splash out and order a
shoulder of lamb for two or foie gras.

CHABROT BISTROT D'AMIS 9 KNIGHTSBRIDGE GREEN SW1X 7QL
020 7225 2238 | CHABROT.COM

28 *Watch the world go by*

Traditional French café open seven days a week.
Great selection of 'croques' and sandwiches, steak
tartare and cassoulet. Black and white chequered floor,
mirrors and French paintings, terrace on the Square.

COLBERT 50-52 SLOANE SQUARE SW1W 8AX
020 7730 2804 | COLBERTCHELSEA.COM

29 *Kitchen theatre*

Smart yet pricey fare by food alchemist Heston Blumenthal. Menu inspired by historic British gastronomy. Book a table near the kitchen to watch chefs at work in the hi-tech kitchen.

DINNER BY HESTON BLUMENTHAL MANDARIN ORIENTAL HYDE PARK, 66 KNIGHTSBRIDGE SW1X 7LA

020 7201 3833 | DINNERBYHESTON.COM

30 *Refined British cooking*

Elegant British cooking with an emphasis on native British produce. Chelsea townhouse with light oak floorboards, pale lemon leather chairs and linen makes for a sumptuous and comfy formal setting.

THE FIVE FIELDS 8-9 BLACKLANDS TERRACE SW3 2SP

020 7838 1082 | FIVEFIELDSRESTAURANT.COM

31 *Local Italian*

Buzzy Italian with plenty of contemporary influences on the menu from Locatelli alumni. Smart location among antique shops attracts elegant clientele. Bare red-brick walls and low-key lighting creates an understated environment.

TINELLO 87 PIMLICO ROAD SW1W 8PH

020 7730 3663 | TINELLO.CO.UK

32 *Fine Italian wines*

A specially designed two-floor Italian wine shop; upstairs houses north Italian wines, downstairs from the south. Polished concrete floors and shelving, spiral staircase, space for tastings and two Enomatic machines to try small measures of wines.

VINI ITALIANI 72 OLD BROMPTON ROAD SW7 3LQ

020 7225 2283 | VINI-ITALIANI.CO.UK

Place to sleep? 33

THE AMPERSAND HOTEL AMPERSANDHOTEL.COM

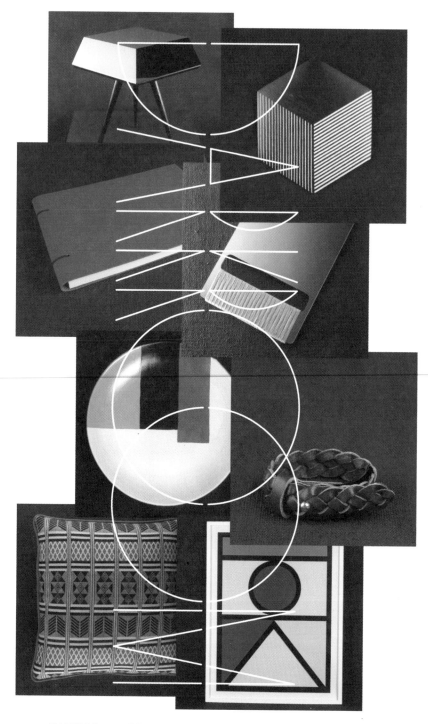

DARKROOM — ACCESSORIES FOR MEN, WOMEN AND THE HOME
52 LAMB'S CONDUIT STREET, LONDON WC1N 3LL
SHOP ONLINE AT WWW.DARKROOMLONDON.COM

THE AGE OF

Considered Consumption

NEIL SAUNDERS

*The one constant in retail is change. The very direct relationship
with consumers means that the sector is always in the vanguard
of shifts in economics, society and culture as it constantly
tries to adapt and remould itself to the emerging shape of
demand. Over the past five years, the pace of change
has become more rapid and its impact more
intense. Retailers of today, be they big or
small, have to think and move
much faster just to
survive*

.

As an outward facing sector, the evidence of this retail change is plain to see. The recent list of failures reads like a roll call of retail powerhouses that, ten or so years ago, looked unassailable. It stands as a testament to the fact that not even the mighty retailers are immune from the shifting laws of demand. At the same time, new players like Amazon have grown rapidly and now rival even retail behemoths like Tesco and Walmart. On a personal level, our own consumption habits, specifically how and where we buy things, are markedly different to how they were just ten short years ago.

It is often tempting to link many of the shifts in retail to the global downturn that began in 2008. Certainly, this has played an important role in reshaping the sector, but its impact should not be overstated. If anything, it has acted as a rather inconvenient catalyst, speeding up existing trends that were already in play, rather than being the architect of change itself. As such, those expecting 'business as usual' once the downturn finally ends are likely to be disappointed. Many of the things impacting on retail today are not aberrations; they are the new normal and will be with us for many years to come.

One of the most profound changes is our attitude to shopping. In the ten years prior to the recession most consumers were profligate – splashing out on this, that and the other with relatively little regard to the cost. Times back then were easy: house prices were rising, credit was cheap, and confidence was high. Combined, they all helped to underpin a boom in retail spending where annual growth averaged out at a very healthy 4.5% each year. As we now know all too well, such a trend was financially unsustainable; but it goes beyond finance – it was psychologically unsustainable, too.

Today, many consumers are jaded with shopping; that doesn't mean they don't like doing it, but that they don't get as much satisfaction out of it as they once did. Today, many consumers are saturated with product, they have homes crammed full of stuff; which doesn't mean that they won't buy new things, but it does mean they think more carefully about what they are buying. These two dynamics, which have partly come about as a reaction against the pre-recession consumer boom, have given rise to a different consumer mindset. As a result of this, and of financial

pressures, the predominant pattern of consumption has evolved into one that is much more considered.

Considered consumption is characterised by a shopper who is less concerned with the pure acquisition of products per se and is more concerned about the nature of those products and their real value. The considered consumer is less impulse driven and questions much more before they buy. Do they really need the item they are buying? Why is it worth the money? What is the quality like? How long will it last? And so forth.

Considered consumption is also a much more holistic form of purchasing. Considered consumers are not only concerned with the product itself, but also with the realities behind it – the ethical soundness of the supply chain, the environment in which the product is sold, and the corporate responsibility of the company that sells it.

Considered consumption is a slower form of buying behaviour. It is less about volume purchasing – that is buying lots of things just because they are cheap – and more about selective purchasing where fewer, perhaps more expensive, items are selected because of their quality or value to the consumer. As consumers become choosier, aggregate demand will continue to weaken and, comparative to historical standards, rates of growth in retail expenditure will be slower. Adapting to this slower growth will be a challenge for many of the big high street names.

On its own, this shift in consumer demand would be challenging enough. However, it is joined by what is quite possibly the most

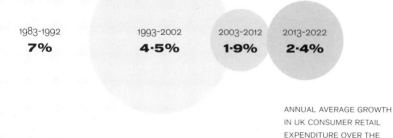

1983-1992
7%

1993-2002
4·5%

2003-2012
1·9%

2013-2022
2·4%

ANNUAL AVERAGE GROWTH
IN UK CONSUMER RETAIL
EXPENDITURE OVER THE
LAST FOUR DECADES

Considered
consumption is
characterised
by a shopper who
is less concerned
with the pure
acquisition of
products per
se and is more
concerned about
the nature of
those products
and their
real value

important retail challenge of the era: the rise of online. In 2007, online accounted for just 4.9% of all retail spending; today, its share is approaching 12% and still rising. By 2020, it could reach as much as 20% of all sales.

From a retail perspective, the internet has brought myriad of benefits. It has allowed retailers to reach new customers and markets, it has given customers more choice than ever before, and it has made things so much more convenient. However, it has not been without its challenges. It has increased competition, made price comparisons a lot easier, and has forced retailers to rethink their business models.

It is important to remember that most of the retail sector as it stands today was conceived and built in a pre-internet era, at a time when stores were needed to reach customers and to act as the point of transaction and exchange. Today that rule no longer holds true. That it doesn't is one of the reasons there is so much reconfiguration across the sector; it's one of the reasons why many retailers are now looking at downsizing their store portfolios with the consequence of pushing up vacancy rates across many high streets.

Downsizing store estates is a relatively obvious reaction to the rise of online. However, it is important not to take the trend to extremes. All too often headlines abound with the news of the death of the high street and the end of physical retail. What these inaccurate predictions often forget is that many stores do have a purpose beyond being places of transaction; they fulfil social functions that online and remote shopping struggle to replicate. As true as this is, however, retailers will need to evolve in their response to both the rise of online and, indeed, to the changing consumer mindset.

The first lesson is that good shops are not warehouses; they do not necessarily need to carry massive assortments. The internet, as a collective entity, provides more choice and variety than any retailer ever could, and it does this efficiently and effectively. Shops need to be different. Arguably, the job of a store is now to curate assortment, to put together a meaningful selection of products that are relevant, interesting and stimulating for consumers. Of course, the exact configuration will vary depending on target audience, competition and location, but the principle holds true across most sectors of retailing.

The second lesson follows closely on from the first. Retailers

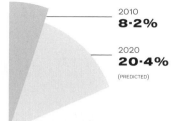

2010
8·2%

2020
20·4%
(PREDICTED)

need to ensure that value is added to the retail offer and to goods in order to give consumers compelling reasons to buy. In a world where we are saturated with product, we will increasingly only buy new things if there is good reason for us to do so. That reason is the value a retailer, or manufacturer, adds. It could take the shape of new functionality, a different design, or a specific benefit. Offers without this inherent added value will, more and more, be forced to compete on price, which is a poor differentiator and will serve only to erode margins.

PROPORTION OF TOTAL UK RETAIL
EXPENDITURE MADE ONLINE

A third lesson is that successful physical stores will need to engage with consumers far more. Outside of grocery retail, the days when retailers could simply put products on shelves and expect them to sell have largely gone. Retailers that create interesting environments that stimulate consumers and give them a reason to visit their stores will be the ones that are able to secure footfall. Part of this is aesthetic: it's about how products are displayed, curated and presented to the consumer and how this changes and evolves over time to keep the store feeling fresh. Part of it is concerned with interaction: it's about customer service, events and advice.

These are not, of course, the only three things retailers need to think about; however, they are important considerations which will, increasingly, mark the difference between success and failure. What's most interesting is that the retailers in the best position to respond to these lessons, and therefore, to attune themselves to the new shape of demand, are not necessarily the big powerhouses, but smaller entities, including many independents. Their nimbleness, their strong links with customers, and the passion of their owners for the products they sell, can be leveraged to great advantage.

These are dramatic times for retail and there can be no doubt that the sector is undergoing a fundamental reconfiguration. The consequences are occasionally painful, sometimes exciting, and always challenging. Those retailers that rise to the challenge, who rethink and renew the way they do business, will be the ones who emerge as the success stories of tomorrow.

Neil Saunders is Managing Director of retail research agency Conlumino
CONLUMINO.COM

Notting Hill
& Ladbroke Grove

W2
W.10
W11

Street*wise*

When did you move to this street?
We first opened our shop on the corner of Golborne and Portobello Roads in September 2011.

What originally attracted you to it?
I've known about Golborne Road since I first left college. I lived behind Porchester Road baths and used to go up to Portobello Road for shopping in the market. Golborne Road was always a bit different and has retained the separation I feel. It still has strong individual communities rubbing along side-by-side, as well as truly independent traders and shopkeepers.

How has this shopping thoroughfare changed since you've been here?
It's always going to change and evolve, just like anywhere else. I regret the closing of a couple of the Moroccan supermarkets, but welcome design shops like Lali and some good new cafés.

What does the street offer the community that is unique?
There is true variety and great value foodwise, as well as a vocal and opinionated community. Although varied and ethnically separate, everyone seems to share and appreciate the thriving pavement life.

Tell us about some of your neighbouring hotspots.
The Moroccan Soup Stand is my number one food stall. Lowry & Baker is great for brunch, coffee and home baking. All of the Portuguese cafés are great, and the fish shop, too. Pizza East has great dinners and the 5x15 events at the Tabernacle in Powis Square are very stimulating. There are a good number of well-curated vintage clothes shops, which I cannot resist. Also, Erno Deco for amazing antique finds. The presence of music store Rough Trade means that Jarvis Cocker is a regular, and we do get some famous faces around the place.

What has recently changed on neighbouring roads that has alarmed you?
Well, the business rates are high in Kensington & Chelsea and that's always a threat to this kind of community. Eventually the high street giants may pile in.

If you could change one thing on the street, what would it be?
We need more benches for people to sit on and eat their lunch! We constantly have people coming in and thanking us for having a bench outside, although our first bench was nicked!

Alison Lloyd
Ally Capellino

312 PORTOBELLO ROAD W10 5RU
020 8964 1022 ALLYCAPELLINO.CO.UK

GOLBORNE ROAD

01 FLOW

📪 1-5 NEEDHAM ROAD W11 2RP

📞 020 7243 0782

↖ FLOWGALLERY.CO.UK

🕐 MON-SAT 11-6

⊖ NOTTING HILL GATE

There are few neighbourhoods that could sustain a meticulously designed shop of this size, in this obscure a corner, selling crafts of such a high order. Flow is a point of pride for Notting Hill residents, however; they've been coming here for gifts and décor and a quiet mooch since Yvonna Demczynska opened in 1999, and the size, scope, design and calibre of the contents are precisely what appeals. Flow offers an uplifting shopping experience devoid of the clutter, crowds and clamour Notting Hill is known for.

Demczynska's early career at the Design and Craft Councils helped build her appreciation for art made with integrity and pure love of the form. She personally seeks out fledgling artists not only from the UK but also abroad, featuring the finest works in bimonthly exhibitions themed by material, colour and subject matter. One recent exhibition highlighted works of wood, ceramic, textiles and jewellery inspired by the written word.

It's essential to view the works up close here; things aren't necessarily as they seem. Ceramics resemble paper, and vice versa. Jewellery and textiles overlap. Barry Griffiths' handcrafted wire tables are ethereal sculptural forms. Cecilia Levy's paper thistles cannily reveal messages from poetic verse. Discovery is part of the joy here – and the opportunity to chat with the owner, often on the premises.

02 MADE.COM

🡒 NEWCOMBE HOUSE, 45 NOTTING HILL GATE W11 3LQ

☎ 0845 557 6888

🡔 MADE.COM

🕐 MON-FRI 11:30-7.30, SAT-SUN 11-5

⊖ NOTTING HILL GATE

The entry to Made.com's new showroom is what you might call 'business casual': up a concrete staircase to the foyer of a nondescript 1960s highrise, where a complicated electronic check-in process… fails to let you in. No matter, you may encounter a pair of jolly employees coming back from lunch, who will escort you to the ninth-floor space and show you around to boot.

Everyone – from the receptionists and the salesmen to the hunky guys hauling around displays – has a jolly demeanour at Made, the young online made-to-order furniture biz that passes on savings from its no-warehouse, no-middle man approach to retail. Like one of those 'best workplaces' listed each year in magazines, the start-up, founded in 2010 by Ning Li and backed by Brent Hoberman, seems to wear its casual mantle with pride, and that attitude extends to its products. The company recruits local jobbing designers like James Harrison, John Stefanidis, and even 'home guru' Alison Cork to fashion fresh, funky pieces in trendy colours, then has them produced in batches of seven when the orders come in.

Items like the £399 red-painted walnut *Fonteyn* dressing table by Steuart Padwick won't change the world, but it may save a young couple who would otherwise be using a milk crate, and possibly become a cherished piece. For a few years, at least.

Founded in 2001 by Marcel Wanders and Casper Vissers, Moooi is named after the Dutch word for beautiful (mooi) with an 'o' added to represent extra value. The designs – by Wanders and contemporary legends like Jurgen Bey and Jaime Hayon – are best known for their dynamism and unique brand of cheek. A Moooi item is never simply 'there'. It winks at you from a mischievous stance. But its UK flagship, a spacious, canal-side Grade II-listed stucco house, gives each item room to express itself. Getting in takes some effort; outside Fridays it's not always certain the lovely staff will answer the phone or the gate. And this is a place for looking only; buyers are directed to Moooi distributors. But do come and look.

The first surprise is the trompe l'oeil resin flooring designed by Wanders and produced by Senso, which shares the showroom. Inside two lofty exhibition rooms the audacious collection is displayed on plinths like museum pieces. The *Altdeutsche* grandfather clock by Studio Job, handpainted in sassy homage to the Frankish style, recently posed with two giant curly brackets mounted at either side. A cluster of *Juuyo* ceramic geisha lamps by Lorenza Bozzoli, Ron Gilad's arachnoid *Dear Ingo* chandelier, and a shiny leather *Golden Chair* by Nika Zupanc all were here. Outrageous, you'll find yourself thinking all too often, but outrageously comfortable, too.

03 MOOOI

- THE WHITE BUILDING, 555 HARROW ROAD W10 4RH
- 020 8962 5691
- MOOOI.COM
- MON-THU 9-5 BY APPOINTMENT, FRI 10-5
- KENSAL GREEN

While disillusioned youngsters and hipsters rally against big branded merchandise, consumer historian Robert Opie sees the necessity – and the beauty – in them. He brought his vast collection of boxes and tins, magazines and adverts, souvenirs and stickers to this space from its Gloucester location nearly 10 years ago to tell the story of our social history. Understandably, it was not difficult to get sponsorship.

It's a charming space, in this mews next to Alice Temperley's fashion showroom. A dark 'time tunnel' of exhibition rooms features a selection of Opie's 12,000 products, plus a series of ever-changing exhibitions on subjects that invariably reveal more than they suggest: wartime labels, sustainable packaging and royal souvenirs among them. Get your nostalgia on here, satisfy your hankering for vintage candy at the museum shop, then traipse through the market stalls at Portobello for something similar to take home.

04 MUSEUM OF BRANDS

- 2 COLVILLE MEWS, LONSDALE ROAD W11 2AR
- 020 7908 0880
- MUSEUMOFBRANDS.COM
- TUE-SAT 10-6, SUN 11-5
- NOTTING HILL GATE

05 THE RUG COMPANY
- 124 HOLLAND PARK AVENUE W11 4LN
- 020 7908 9990
- THERUGCOMPANY.COM
- MON-SAT 10-6, SUN 11-5
- HOLLAND PARK

It's known for its big-name collaborations, magazine mentions and high prices, but there's a reason for all that. The Rug Company is like the Sherpa of quality craftsmanship, hauling Tibetan-wool rugs, hand-dyed and hand-knotted over several months, from Kathmandu to the hub of affluent London. The process is almost satirically compassionate, involving mountain-dwelling sheep and Tibetan artisans fairly paid to preserve traditional rug-making techniques. But beyond all that is the superlative design, fascinating patterns that take your breath away. Like a canvas or tapestry that becomes the focal point of a room, these rugs can cost in the thousands of pounds, but if you have one, there's no need for any other ornamentation.

Founders Suzanne and Christopher Sharp have become veritable celebrities for their successful alliances with designers like Paul Smith, Matthew Williamson and Barber Osgerby. They were one of the first importers to help underfoot design transcend the tired patterns of hotels and banks. And in the process, they also popularised traditional Berber and Turkish kilim styles. You'll find those here, neatly stacked on shelves in surprising contemporary colours or rolled in the corner with their tassels aloft. But you'll fall for (or literally onto) the oversized florals and snazzy geometrics of the 'designer' rugs, each of which comes with a handy postcard to take home and debate over with your partner.

06 SCP WEST
- 87 WESTBOURNE GROVE W2 4UL
- 020 7229 3612
- SCP.CO.UK
- MON 10-6, TUE-SAT 9:30-6, SUN 11-5
- BAYSWATER/QUEENSWAY

While SCP's original store (p.159) on Shoreditch's gritty Curtain Road has been trading since 1985, this low glass box on the busy end of Westbourne Grove is 22 years its junior. A fraction of the size of its East End parent and seemingly more busy as a result, this store caters for the burgeoning appetite for contemporary design on this side of the city. The stock differs too, with more emphasis on smaller items and giftware and lighter on major furnishings. Regardless, it carries a Best Of selection that could easily consume a lunch hour or more.

The highlights include Kay + Stemmer's modern-classic *Agnes* range of oak and walnut console tables and shelving, with those irresistible tapered legs; braided rugs by Donna Wilson; and David Chipperfield's triumphant brass table lamp, built with no visible joints. The children's section elicits a chorus of *oohs* and *awwwws* and has even bachelors stocking up on gifts. And give me a Jansen + Co cake stand from the china section any day of the week.

07 THEMES & VARIATIONS

- 231 WESTBOURNE GROVE W11 2SE
- 020 7727 5531
- THEMESANDVARIATIONS.COM
- MON–FRI 10-1, 2-6; SAT 10-6
- NOTTING HILL GATE

Before the movie and the blue door or even some of you, dear readers, there was Themes & Variations, which bet its shirt (or, rather, the savings of dealer Liliane Fawcett) on the area's economic arrival. If London is having a love affair with European contemporary postwar design, Fawcett was the matchmaker.

This is where Piero Fornasetti made his name in London design circles. A prolific and much reproduced sensation, Fornasetti is less known for his fantastically complicated bureaus and desks, which come to Fawcett's shop at regular intervals. I have thrice spotted a Fornasetti trumeau in store, each a different style, each with doors, shelves, desks and hidden compartments – justifying the price, that of a small flat.

Of course there are other wonders here: Fontana Arte floor lamps and Gio Ponti wing chairs. And, for fans of the contemporary, there is Cedric Ragot's limited-edition gold *Hyperfast* vase, a casting feat, and McCollin Bryan's cast-resin tables. It's a sparsely furnished space, however, and stock moves quickly. Recently, after picking up a leaflet featuring an antique Chinese chair adorned in pom-poms by Shanghai artist Gu Yeli, I then found it wrapped up and ready to go out the door.

08 TOM DIXON SHOP

- PORTOBELLO DOCK, 344 LADBROKE GROVE W10 5BU
- 020 7400 0500
- TOMDIXON.NET
- MON–SAT 10-6, SUN 11-5
- LADBROKE GROVE/KENSAL GREEN

'Why don't I come here more often?' is the thought I have each time I make it to Portobello Dock. Not that I don't get enough of Tom Dixon – he is ubiquitous on the London design trail. The canal setting, rather, is the thing here. Just north of the interesting bit of Portobello Road, Dixon's converted warehouse (look for the Innocent smoothie symbol on the neighbouring headquarters) has atmosphere in spades. Dark and broody, the showroom glows in places from the designer's trendsetting metallic lighting and a curious cluster of ceramic lustre pendants, each hand-cast with a unique iridescent sheen.

His furniture collection is here too, impossibly smooth wood chairs and benches and upholstered pieces with almost Art Deco curvaceousness. They're styled against metallic vessels and giftware like the cast-iron brogue doorstop and stoneware kitchen gadgets, plus inspiring items from fellow designers that Dixon curates with a gallerist's eye. Wander around the site and you'll spot his stacking chairs and offcut stools by windows overlooking the canal towpath. And since you're making the trip, book a table at the Dock Kitchen, sited above the showroom and furnished, naturally, with the man's own creations.

09 VESSEL

114 KENSINGTON PARK ROAD W11 2PW

020 7727 8001

VESSELGALLERY.COM

MON–SAT 10–6

NOTTING HILL GATE

It's one of those inexplicable truths that even the most fashionable among us get our tableware from wedding lists or high-street chains – except those among us from Notting Hill. Vessel is a reliable old friend in these parts, scouting out the most original and statement-making china and glassware outside the ateliers of Murano (though they, too, have been commissioned to produce some of the designer collections here). The owners, Nadia Demetriou Ladas and Angel Monzon, do a swift retail business in Fornasetti urns, ceramic mounted horse's heads and paper-thin glass vases that resemble dried fruit pods – not to mention one striking Kosta Boda interpretation of the lawn flamingo. It's the roster of exhibitions, though, that draws in the numbers.

The vast and complicated glass- and ceramic-art worlds are rarely seen, even by dedicated gallery-hoppers, and Vessel gets to the heart of them, showing industry legends like Oiva Toikka, Lena Bergström and Jeremy Maxwell Wintrebert, as well as emerging talents, bringing an element of added value to this snug two-level space. The duo have also helped more mainstream artists launch niche collections, like Jaime Hayon and his Japanese-style tableware, or John Pawson, who did a minimal range of decorative homeware exclusively for Vessel. The company also operates a growing contract business, popular with architects and interior designers.

10 *Alfresco lunch*

Young chef Stevie Parle uses global culinary influences and seasonal produce for his simple yet exciting menu. Light-filled Tom Dixon-designed interior. Great spot on Grand Union canal with peaceful outdoor dining area.

DOCK KITCHEN PORTOBELLO DOCK, 344 LADBROKE GROVE W10 5BU | 020 8962 1610 | DOCKKITCHEN.CO.UK

11 *American appeal*

After a recent refurbishment, the Electric now feels like a proper old American diner. Curved wood-panelled ceiling accentuates the diner feel further; banquettes jut out from the walls, while bar stools line the bar for diners and cocktail lovers.

ELECTRIC DINER 191 PORTOBELLO ROAD W11 2ED 020 7908 9696 | ELECTRICDINER.COM

12 *A sunny breakfast*

Famous Australian chef Bill Granger's first London restaurant. Minimal interior with big panelled windows at this corner site. Food is vibrant and colourful with big flavours. No reservations. Open early until late, expect queues at peak times.

GRANGER & CO 175 WESTBOURNE GROVE W11 2SB 020 7229 8944 | GRANGERANDCO.COM

13 *Best of British*

Former Victorian butcher's shop, now popular neighbourhood spot from ex-St John chef. Classy, American-style leather booths. Distinctly British menu. Good spot for a romantic dinner.

HEREFORD ROAD 3 HEREFORD ROAD W2 4AB 020 7727 1144 | HEREFORDROAD.ORG

14 Gastronomic dinner

Elegant, smart culinary gem, often remarked as
the best restaurant in London, two Michelin stars.
Gastronomic cuisine is inventive, beautiful and a
special treat. A must for food geeks. Outdoor patio
area great in the summer. Pricey.

THE LEDBURY 127 LEDBURY ROAD W11 2AQ

020 7792 9090 | THELEDBURY.COM

15 Top-of-the-range pizza

Now one of three Pizza East restaurants in
London. Occupies a restored Georgian pub.
Stripped-back, textured interior with old industrial
furniture and fittings. Very popular.

PIZZA EAST [PICTURED] 310 PORTOBELLO ROAD W10 5TA

020 8969 4500 | PIZZAEASTPORTOBELLO.COM

16 The perfect G&T

Unassuming small bar in the heart of the market.
Serves delicious cocktails from expert mixologists
with a particular interest in gin. Range of Ginger Pig
pies sold at lunchtime. Hangout for the bar industry.

PORTOBELLO STAR 171 PORTOBELLO ROAD W11 2DY

020 7229 8016 | PORTOBELLOSTARBAR.CO.UK

17 Rum & jerk

A 1970s tiki lair under Portobello Road. A lounge bar,
den and kitchen serving Caribbean-influenced food.
Try the jerk chicken burger with everything and
cassava chips. Started the Notting Hill Rum Club
and has an impressive list of cocktails.

TRAILER HAPPINESS 177 PORTOBELLO ROAD W11 2DY

020 7313 4664 | TRAILERHAPPINESS.COM

18 Place to sleep?

MILLER'S RESIDENCE MILLERSHOTEL.COM

Shops *make* streets

YVONNE COURTNEY

A period living abroad, in countries where neighbourhoods are next to non-existent, hit home how special London's streets are; exploring the city's diverse shopping areas was one of the things I missed most about not being in London.

Speaking about our bricks and mortar retailers, retail guru Mary Portas puts it particularly succinctly: "use them or lose them!" While her campaign is for the nation's high streets, this guide's call is more niche: cherish and nourish London's cult shopping destinations if you don't want to be left with online or Westfield as your only options.

After all, shops do more than simply sell stuff. They create places where people want to meet, hang out with friends, get things cleaned or repaired, or simply pass the time. They are places where you get to know the shopkeepers and service providers, who can play a key role in local communities – and therefore our lives. Without that, we would lose our sense of belonging, and a social infrastructure that is vital to us as human beings.

It might be easier these days to slot in some online retail therapy between work and play... but nothing beats a leisurely stroll around one of London's shopping nooks, stumbling across a cluster of outlets, all there to be discovered.

Many of London's neighbourhood enclaves have become desirable shopping destinations in their own right, such as those highlighted here: Lamb's Conduit Street, Elystan Street, Chiltern Street, Mount Street, Great Titchfield Street, Redchurch Street, Exmouth Market, Golborne Road, Bermondsey Street, Camden Passage and Lower Marsh.

From the splendid grandeur of Mayfair's Mount Street to the quirky eclecticism of Waterloo's Lower Marsh, these shopping destinations are extremely diverse, yet share certain ingredients, which make these vibrant hubs so attractive and full of character.

While most are distinctly middle class, they are places where people from all social groups would feel comfortable and have reason to go there. Another recurring feature is that these streets aren't overrun with global brands, instead featuring independent stores which are thriving. To add to the mix, a lot of

Shops do more than simply sell stuff. They create places where people want to meet, hang out with friends, get things cleaned or repaired, or simply pass the time

these streets also have a market and are pedestrianised or have restricted access to vehicles.

These areas have been built to a human scale, which is instinctively appealing, and the properties are spatially and financially more conducive for small businesses. The areas tend to feature specialist or niche services alongside shops and eateries, making for a more fulfilling and rewarding experience.

However, a by-product of successful shopping enclaves are the dangers that gentrification brings. This was witnessed with the changing face of Westbourne Grove, which ten years ago was a design destination, filled with galleries, antiques dealers, furniture outlets and showrooms, but has since become a predictable fashion strip for Notting Hill's smug hedge fund-financed families.

This threat currently looms over Redchurch Street, partly triggered by the opening of the Boundary Hotel and Shoreditch House. The arrival of brands like APC, Jack Wills and Boxpark have signalled the departure of the outfits that made the area so edgy and unique in the first place.

This is a pattern being repeated across town, couched in developerspeak cliches like 'regeneration', 'flagship', and 'public realm enhancements'. No sooner praising an area's special identity, developers, estate agents and landlords proceed to banish all character, rendering it virtually unrecognisable.

Of course, progress is inevitable. Cities can't stand still. Attempts to resist the might of the developers to protect local character and history merely results in the preservation in aspic of an idealised past that possibly never really existed.

In the meantime, there are an increasing number of initiatives that seek to highlight an area's USP. Clerkenwell Design Week, Brompton Design District, South London Art Map, Fitzrovia Now design trail and Hackney Wicked are all attempts by local businesses and players to create or cement a concept of community – both within the neighbourhood and in the wider domain. Some have been enormously beneficial in establishing a new reputation for a particular postcode. However, they risk laying the foundation for developers to exploit the area's individuality, inflating residential prices and commercial rents in the process.

Shops impose a sense of identity onto a locality, providing a social anchor in our day-to-day lives. So it is up to us, the consumer, to play a part in supporting these special places and spaces, the heartbeats of London's evolving communities.

Yvonne Courtney is a design PR advisor, retail & cultural broker, curator and writer
DESIGNTASTIC.NET

Another Country

Contemporary Craft Furniture

anothercountry.com

Marylebone

W1

BAKER ST

MARYLEBONE RD

EUSTON RD

REGENT'S PARK

LUXBOROUGH ST
NOTTINGHAM PL
DEVONSHIRE PL
HARLEY ST

02

CHILTERN ST

PADDINGTON ST

03

DEVONSHIRE ST

PORTLAND PL

07

BAKER ST

400M DORSET ST

14

09
16 15
MOXON ST

MARYLEBONE HIGH ST

CRAMER ST

20

ST VINCENT ST

WEYMOUTH ST

WESTMORELAND ST

WIMPOLE ST

WIMPOLE MEWS

HARLEY ST

17

18

NEW CAVENDISH ST

BLANDFORD ST

13
04

GEORGE ST

MANCHESTER ST

21

PORTLAND PL

GREAT PORTLAND ST

MANCHESTER

HINDE ST

SQ

11

06

MANDEVILLE PL

MARYLEBONE LN

19
10 12

WELLBECK ST

WIMPOLE ST

BULSTRODE ST

QUEEN ANNE ST

WIGMORE ST

CAVENDISH

MORTIMER ST

ORCHARD ST

BARRETT ST

DUKE ST

BIRD ST

JAMES ST

ST CHRISTOPHER'S PL

05

GEES CT

01

MARYLEBONE LN

HENRIETTA PL

CHAPEL PL

VERE ST

OLD CAVENDISH ST

SQ

HOLLES ST

LITTLE PORTLAND

MARGARET ST

REGENT ST

EASTCASTLE ST

08

OXFORD ST

Mayfair | p.066

BOND ST

OXFORD CIRCUS

● *Design galleries & institutions*
● *Design shops & C20th vintage*

● *Eat & drink (pp.060-061)*

01 BOFFI WIGMORE
02 THE CONRAN SHOP
03 DESIGNER'S GUILD
04 LAGO BAKER STREET
05 MARIMEKKO
06 OTHER CRITERIA
07 RIBA
08 SELFRIDGES & CO
09 SKANDIUM

10 TRACY NEULS
11 VITSŒ

Street*wise*

When did you move to this street?
When I launched menswear store Trunk in September 2010.

What originally attracted you to it?
I wanted to be in Marylebone and somewhere off the main high street to make Trunk more of a destination. Chiltern Street is a very defined space, with the red brick residential buildings on either side and the very beautiful fire station now being turned into a hotel by André Balazs.

How has this street changed since you've been here?
Chiltern Street has always been, and will most likely continue to be, a fairly quiet street. This is what gives it the charm that streets like Oxford Street or Regent Street lack. The opening of the Monocle Café has made a big difference and I, like everyone else on the street, am now very much looking forward to seeing how the hotel right across the street from Trunk will change things.

What does the street offer the community that is unique?
There is an eclectic mix of independent retailers for both men and women - some that have been there for over 35 years and some just for a couple of months. There are also no chain stores in sight, which I think is rather rare these days.

Tell us about some of your neighbouring hotspots.
Monocle Café for my morning flat white, Il Baretto on Blandford Street for lunch and drinks, and dinner at The Providores on Marylebone High Street.

What has recently changed on neighbouring roads that has alarmed you?
Most developments in the area are positive and there's an initiative backed by various stakeholders to make the area surrounding Baker Street more of a destination than just an area you travel through to get from A to B. Luckily, Trunk hasn't been impacted, but there's been some break-ins in the area, which naturally is a bit worrying.

If you could change one thing on the street, what would it be?
I'd put some more trees on it! Trees and greenery in general make any street so much more welcoming. In terms of other retailers, I think it would be great if a nice baker came to the street, a florist with a great selection, and maybe a bookshop, too.

Mats Klingberg
Trunk

8 CHILTERN STREET W1U 7PU
020 7486 2357 TRUNKCLOTHIERS.COM

CHILTERN STREET

01 BOFFI WIGMORE

25 WIGMORE STREET W1U 1PN
020 7629 0058
BOFFIUK.COM
MON–SAT 9:30–5:30
BOND STREET

The strip of Wigmore Street above Bond Street tube can be sterile in parts, for all the medical suppliers, hair salons and kitchen retailers, but the latter are becoming more alluring, thanks to the recent arrival of Boffi, which alters perceptions of what a kitchen should be. This sumptuous space, a former bank now wrapped in luxurious charcoal panelling and accessorised with homely leather furnishings, bamboo and a statement chandelier, is designed by the legendary Milanese architect and designer Piero Lissoni, who has spent decades ensuring the brand is the nonpareil of utilitarian design.

The kitchens here on the main floor, as well as the bathrooms below, are so wily with storage and hidden hardware, so richly surfaced, that you hardly seem to know what sort of a room you're looking at. Which is, of course, the point. Lissoni and his designers – luminaries like Naoto Fukasawa, Claudio Silvestrin and Marcel Wanders – have brought us to the point where we need never again gaze upon unsightly plumbing or extractors if we can afford not to.

We don't include the 'permanents' for the home – kitchens and bathrooms – in this guide, but we make an exception here as this showroom is worth a look for the fantasy alone.

02 THE CONRAN SHOP MARYLEBONE

55 MARYLEBONE HIGH STREET W1U 5HS

020 7723 2223

CONRANSHOP.CO.UK

MON-WED, FRI 10-6, THU 10-7, SAT 10-6:30, SUN 11-5

BAKER STREET

These former stables at the top of Marylebone High Street have been overhauled, emptied out and given a lick of sharp white paint. You'll probably notice that the contents of the ground and first floors have been flipped, so the latest accessories and giftware have been brought down to the ground where they belong and the hulking seating moved upstairs, making the space more open and navigable. Adding to the appeal, for parents at least, is a cheerful children's section and a welcoming café.

Upstairs, along with the more substantial pieces, is the company's Found collection of restored vintage – when I last looked, a pair of schoolroom chairs with built-in desks for £295 apiece. And the calming top floor, with its sectional sofas from the Conran label and designers like Cini Boeri and Piero Lissoni, has the look of an apartment, complete with kitchen.

The Conran Shop's founder Terence Conran is the godfather of contemporary design retail in Britain. He went from being a small-scale entrepreneur in the 1960s to spawning conglomerates of furniture and restaurant businesses. Without him, well-made contemporary design might've been totally unattainable. His son, Jasper, is now the chairman and creative director of The Conran Shop and can be thanked for sustaining the vision and adding an injection of energy that makes their shops more appealing than ever.

03 DESIGNERS GUILD

- ➤ 76 MARYLEBONE HIGH STREET W1U 5JU
- ☎ 020 3301 5826
- ➤ DESIGNERSGUILD.COM
- 🕐 MON–SAT 10–6, SUN 11–5
- ⊖ BOND STREET/BAKER STREET

Walk into these bijou premises and you wouldn't naturally assume the owner was a force to be reckoned with. Like a conservatory where everything is for sale, Designers Guild surrounds you with fresh colour, natural fabrics, antique-like pottery and a bouquet of floral scents. And yet the woman behind it, Tricia Guild, has spent 40-something years building an industry of retail and wholesaling that employs hundreds in the UK and abroad. Guild has a sixth sense for colour, managing always to keep a step ahead of trends to bring you what you didn't know you had to have. As a result, her linens, wallpapers and upholsteries have an uncanny modernity where others' might descend into chintz.

The expansive King's Road flagship (p.017) is a rush – it hits you from all directions. This one grows on you more subtly – indeed, you might fully walk past it, like I did, believing it's a florist. But stick with it. You'll start to get the colour combinations, rethink your bathroom scheme and possibly even find a deal.

04 LAGO BAKER STREET

- ➤ 55 BAKER STREET W1U 8EW
- ☎ 020 7486 0311
- ➤ LONDON-BAKERSTREET.LAGOSTORE.NET
- 🕐 MON–SAT 9–6, THU 9–8, SUN 12–5
- ⊖ BAKER STREET

When a retailer turns up a winning formula, he'd better maximise the benefit. And so the small design chain Living Space has streamlined its offerings and renamed itself Lago, after the Padua-based designer Daniele Lago, who has expanded his repertoire to include not only shelving systems and barely-there bed frames but a complete range of interior architecture – kitchen sink included.

Baker Street was the first Living Space to go the Lago way, and it exists now as a flagship for London, a living catalogue for how the brand can free up your space and create a place for all your stuff (mind you, Lago lovers aren't big fans of stuff). The designer is a proponent of horizontal space, and walking through this location is like occupying a Mondrian. The most prevalent shelving line, *Linea*, can be pieced together in any configuration, with doors or without, in colours you wouldn't believe, the horizontal motifs created by positive or negative space.

It's not all sterile. Lago's affinity for matt oak is manifested in his *Wildwood* range of tables that can be sliced to fit and equipped with storage. The wood makes the look increasingly liveable, even when set on transparent legs. Even when the *Weightless* range of ceiling-anchored shelving is bearing down on you.

There is a rainbow at the end of skinny St Christopher's Place, a gem of a lane between the ambitious flagships of Oxford and Wigmore Streets. You could never blame Marimekko, the august Finnish textile designer, for putting you in a grumpy mood, though you could fault it for verging on the twee. The boldest, jolliest prints this side of the Baltic Sea can be found in this Scandi-white boutique, some tailored into pretty sundresses, emblazoned onto teapots or fashioned into bags, others simply folded in reams you can pull out for full impact.

You may recognise the popular flower motifs from your own toddlerhood – a couple have been reproduced consistently since the company's inception in the 1950s. But new classics are being created all the time now, on contemporary homewares, fashion-forward trenchcoats, even Plimsols. The brand is doing a fine job of profiting from this era of colour, colour, colour – and as a result it's as relevant as ever.

05 MARIMEKKO

- 16-17 ST CHRISTOPHER'S PLACE W1U 1NZ
- 020 7486 6454
- MARIMEKKO.COM
- MON-SAT 10-6:30, SUN 12-5
- BOND STREET

Damien Hirst launched the art publisher Other Criteria in 2005, along with Hugh Allan and his manager Frank Dunphy. The plan was to open a retail location for the books, along with limited-edition *objets*, art and T-shirts from artists big and small. That sliver of a location opened in 2009 here on Hinde Street, a few steps from the Wallace Collection, with art by Jeff Koons, vases by Paola Petrobelli and a porcelain tea set by Cindy Sherman.

Five years later, that impressive roster seems to have stepped aside to make room for Hirst's growing repertoire of spot-covered accessories, glittery skull graphics and butterfly-infested wallpapers (*The Rape of Persephone* being the latest pattern). One wall of books includes titles from Yoko Ono, Mustafa Hulusi and John Isaacs, but Hirst takes up most of the shelves with his numerous monographs. And with the exception of a bong-shaped Murano-glass sculpture by Mat Collishaw, the art is Hirst's, too. I hoped for a cache of surprises on the lower level, reached by a staircase of handsome parquet, but there were more butterflies down there. Nothing wrong with *Spin Painting* flipbooks and rugs, of course, but other artists should see this as an opportunity.

06 OTHER CRITERIA

- 14 HINDE STREET W1U 3BG
- 020 7935 5550
- OTHERCRITERIA.COM
- MON-SAT 10-6
- BOND STREET

 RIBA

66 PORTLAND PLACE W1B 1AD

020 7580 5533

ARCHITECTURE.COM

MON–SAT 10–5

GREAT PORTLAND STREET

The Royal Institute of British Architects has lived on this corner, in this George Grey Wornum-designed art deco pile, for 80 years. You might have thought it would have commissioned new digs by now, by one of its Stirling Prize-awarded architects, for instance. But the government-supported body for architectural standards, excellence and education across the UK can see a good thing when it's inside one. And once you get past the Falun Gong demonstrators on the pavement (focused on the Chinese embassy across the street), you'll agree there are few buildings as inspiring as this in London.

And yet it's not intimidating. In the foyer you'll be greeted with smiles as you inspect the goodies at the café and make your way into the bookshop, resourceful as a library with study manuals all the way through to showy coffee table tomes. Up the grand staircase, two exhibition spaces show a roster of insightful installations: perspectives on Asian architecture, solutions from across Europe and meditations on public housing. In one space is an elegant dining room overlooking the boulevard. And still further, on the third floor, is a library of almost Oxbridge magnificence, open to the public and equipped with literally millions of drawings, photos and archival records.

08 SELFRIDGES & CO
400 OXFORD STREET W1A 1AB
0800 123 400
SELFRIDGES.COM
MON-SAT 9:30-9, SU 11:30-6
BOND STREET/MARBLE ARCH

Retail has so evolved in the past 20 years, walking into the foyer of a department store can make you feel like you're on a *Mad Men* soundstage (all those fragrance pushers!). Selfridges has undoubtedly moved forward in the past decade under the creative directorship of Alannah Weston, yet it does take a trip to the basement homewares department to see real changes.

First it's the colour that gets you: a spectrum in nearly every department, from Joseph Joseph to Le Creuset and Nespresso. Then the variety opens up. There's spanking-new tableware from Tom Dixon, a Skandium concession with an item I couldn't find even at the flagship around the corner (p.058), and replacements for your wedding china. If you're shopping for chintz or workaday linens, you're in the wrong place: beautiful basics are what the fourth floor is for. But if it's the broadest selection of Jonathan Adler outside his Sloane Avenue boutique, or a row of red-velvet vintage theatre seats, or a new coffee table book, the basement is for you.

Service ranges from earnest to snobbish and bored, mind you, and you should never deign to be here on a weekend. But if you do wind up here on a mad Saturday afternoon, hunt out pockets of calm in this monolithic building (such as the fourth floor furniture department) or relax with a glass of vino in Harry Gordon's wine bar in the basement.

09 SKANDIUM

📍 86 MARYLEBONE HIGH STREET W1U 4QS

📞 020 7935 2077

↖ SKANDIUM.COM

🕐 MON-SAT 10-6:30, THU 10-7, SUN 11-5

⊖ BAKER STREET/BOND STREET

British tastes have embraced Scandinavian style so completely in the past few decades that names like Aalto, Jacobsen and Wegner have almost Cher-like recognition. Millions of us own a piece of Scandinavian design (even disregarding IKEA) and umpteen retailers now stock it. Skandium remains king of them all, however. The ever-expanding enterprise defined who's who in the Scandi canon and continues to set a standard with the best new products from the region.

It also redefined retail with its open white-walled spaces flooded with natural light from all aspects; even the basement, dedicated to fabric and hardware, is pleasantly airy. It's no wonder Marylebone High Street seems to have grown up around it. Pieces seem not to take up much weight in material or shape – ideal for small British homes – yet many of them work hard, stacking, swivelling, storing, expanding and contracting. While others, like Vitra's *Corniches* shelves by Ronan and Erwan Bouroullec, and that ubiquitous Rosendahl monkey, simply bring joy. The staff seem to harbour a bit of joy themselves; never idle, they bury themselves in paperwork or unpacking, and yet they're always aware when you need them.

She may be a cobbler but Tracey Neuls's name is as well known in London as some furniture designers. Her TN29 boutique, since opening in 2000, has become a fixture on the Design Festival circuit for her collaborations with design-world names like Nicola Yeoman, Tord Boontje, Moroso and Retrouvius. Even left to her own devices, Neuls's space is a surreal fantasy world. She was one of the first retailers to display wares from the ceiling rather than the floor, dangling her sculptural shoes from undetectable wires.

Initially the point was to exhibit her designs for 360-degree viewing. A TN29 shoe is so detail-oriented, even the sole is stamped with a quirky scene. But that tickled her ever more innovative nose for merchandising, so that you never know what tableau you'll encounter when you visit. The shop itself is also a 360-degree deal. Neuls has been known to bake bread in full view to make you feel at home, and decorate with stylish finds that put this space on a par with the slickest concept shops.

10 TRACEY NEULS
☛ 29 MARYLEBONE LANE W1U 2NQ
☎ 020 7935 0039
↖ TRACEYNEULS.COM
◔ MON-FRI 11-6:30, SAT-SUN 12-5
⊖ BOND STREET

A lot has happened in the 50-odd years since Dieter Rams designed his *606 Universal Shelving System* for Vitsœ, the pinnacle of flexibility and the godfather of modular furnishings. But nothing seems to come close to the efficacy of the pioneer. Trends come, go and come back again and we all cherry-pick according to our preferences. But few people would deny that if they were given a blank slate, they'd start fresh with the *606*.

Available in a range of muted colours, with an even wider range of components that manage to look at once cool and functional for an office and warm and décorative for a lounge, the system is perfection on rails. Which is why the Duke Street showrooms – two sister shops in charming, bow-windowed Arts and Crafts style – are busy from open till close. Staff are less retailers than architects, as open to the possibilities of their product as they are intensely familiar with it. At the end of the day, though, it is just shelving. You may not be yearning for a tour, but taking it instils another sort of yearning.

11 VITSŒ
☛ 3-5 DUKE STREET W1U 3ED
☎ 020 7428 1606
↖ VITSOE.COM
◔ MON-SAT 10-6
⊖ BOND STREET

12 *Fine wines*

Informal wine bar and restaurant; work your way through the great selection of wines by the glass, charcuterie and proper French bistro food. Crates of wine line the walls.

28°-50° WINE WORKSHOP & KITCHEN [PICTURED]
15-17 MARYLEBONE LN W1U 2NE
020 7486 7922 | 2850.CO.UK

● ● ●   ● ●

13 *Quality British fare*

Stunning canteen-style restaurant on busy road. Superb ingredients, no-nonsense menu. Postwar feel with relaxed atmosphere. Ask for booth.

CANTEEN 55 BAKER STREET W1U 8EW
0845 686 1122 | CANTEEN.CO.UK

● ● ●

14 *Dine alone*

Small unassuming Japanese with minimal surroundings, serves Japanese-style tapas, combining traditional Japanese with modern European cuisine. There's a counter to watch chefs at work, perfect for dining alone.

DININGS 22 HARCOURT STREET W1H 4HH
020 7723 0666 | DININGS.CO.UK

● ○ ●   ○ ○ ○

15 *For cheese lovers*

Dedicated dairy, deli and café. Stylish and unconventional with communal eating. Ideal for indulgent lunch or early-afternoon snack. Tantalisingly rich flavours with aroma of freshly baked bread.

LA FROMAGERIE 2-6 MOXON STREET W1U 4EW
020 7935 0341 | LAFROMAGERIE.CO.UK

● ● ●

16 *Top-of-the-range meat*

Proper traditional butcher selling proper quality meat. Produce comes from their own farms. Daily menu of cooked take-home meals. Treat yourself to the aged T-bone.

THE GINGER PIG 8-10 MOXON STREET W1U 4EW
020 7935 7788 | THEGINGERPIG.CO.UK

● ○ ○   ○ ○ ○

17 *Schmooze*

Café from intellectual tome *Monocle*, founded by
Tyler Brulé. Coffee, cakes and expensive chocolate
bars from abroad! Place to hang out, see and be seen.
MONOCLE CAFÉ 18 CHILTERN STREET W1U 7NT
020 7725 4388 | MONOCLE.COM

18 *Discreet café catch-up*

Contemporary café serving simple sweet and
savoury Nordic goods. Calm atmosphere with
minimalist Scandi interior. Highlights are the sticky
cinnamon buns and great coffee.
NORDIC BAKERY 37B NEW CAVENDISH STREET W1G 8JR
020 7935 3590 | NORDICBAKERY.COM

19 *For the perfect cup of tea*

British treasure in Marylebone, established in 1900.
Family-run. Serves a wide variety of teas and English
food. Great selection of jams and relishes for sale.
Polite and welcoming, attracting all sorts.
PAUL ROTHE & SON 35 MARYLEBONE LANE W1U 2NN
020 935 6783

20 *Big flavours*

Formal dining room upstairs, casual tapas café
downstairs. Mediterranean fused with Asian via
New Zealand, sounds odd but it's brilliant. Makes for
a fun culinary romp.
THE PROVIDORES & TAPA ROOM 109 MARYLEBONE HIGH ST
W1U 4RX | 020 7935 6175 | THEPROVIDORES.CO.UK

21 *Indulgent dining*

Michelin-starred Indian with sister restaurant in
Mumbai, focuses on seafood in particular, stunning
dishes simply prepared, this is the next level of
Indian food. Design is minimal; clean lines, exposed
brick and light wooden furniture.
TRISHNA 15-17 BLANDFORD STREET W1U 3DG
020 7935 5624 | TRISHNALONDON.COM

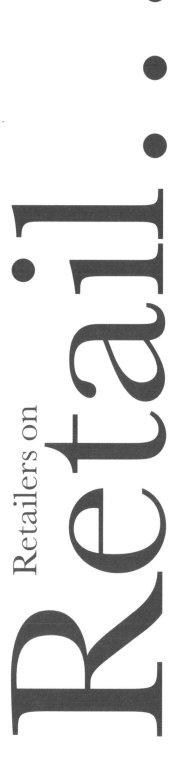

Retailers on

In attendance:

James Mair owner of Viaduct
YEARS IN RETAIL   25
SHOP LOCATION   Clerkenwell
PROPERTY STATUS   owned

Tracey Neuls owner of Tracey Neuls
YEARS IN RETAIL   7
SHOP LOCATIONS   Marylebone and Shoreditch
PROPERTY STATUS   rented

Sheridan Coakley owner of SCP
YEARS IN RETAIL   25
SHOP LOCATIONS   Shoreditch and Notting Hill
PROPERTY STATUS   owned and rented

Magnus Englund co-owner of Skandium
YEARS IN RETAIL   14
SHOP LOCATIONS   Marylebone, Selfridges,
                 Brompton & Fitzrovia
PROPERTY STATUS   rented

Mia Thittichai showroom manager of Knoll
YEARS IN RETAIL   4
SHOP LOCATION   Clerkenwell
PROPERTY STATUS   rented

Justin Pratt manager of KnollStudio, UK
and International
YEARS IN RETAIL   4
SHOP LOCATION   Clerkenwell
PROPERTY STATUS   rented

Rhonda Drakeford co-owner of Darkroom
YEARS IN RETAIL   4
SHOP LOCATION   Bloomsbury
PROPERTY STATUS   rented

Simon Alderson co-owner of Twentytwentyone
YEARS IN RETAIL   17
SHOP LOCATIONS   Islington and Clerkenwell
PROPERTY STATUS   rented and owned

Lina Kanafani owner of Mint
YEARS IN RETAIL   15
SHOP LOCATION   Brompton
PROPERTY STATUS   rented

Also joined by retail analyst **Neil Saunders**,
managing director of Conlumino

Hosted by **Max Fraser** editor
of *London Design Guide*

Analysts assess, media speculates and the rest of us all have an opinion. But what do the retailers themselves have to say about the changing face of their business? We invited a handful of London's leading design retailers to openly discuss the pressures and the opportunities of trading today.

PREMISES, RENTS & RATES

MAX FRASER

It strikes me that those of you who have been in business for the longest also own your properties. Is that what you put your long-term survival down to?

JAMES MAIR

Yes, I think it was one of those decisions that has given us security and allowed us to take more risks.

MAX FRASER

Does anyone here who is renting see rent hikes as one of the biggest risks to their business model?

LINA KANAFANI

Well, it's the biggest expense: when things are not so good, it is a pressure. And then the moment you get going, you get a rent review every five years.

Continued p.074

HANNAH MARTIN

ICONIC FINE JEWELLERY HANDMADE IN LONDON

SHOP ONLINE AT **HANNAHMARTINLONDON.COM** OR AT THE PRIVATE SHOWROOM
PLEASE CALL 020 3302 1964 FOR ALL ENQUIRIES AND APPOINTMENTS

Mayfair

W1
SW1

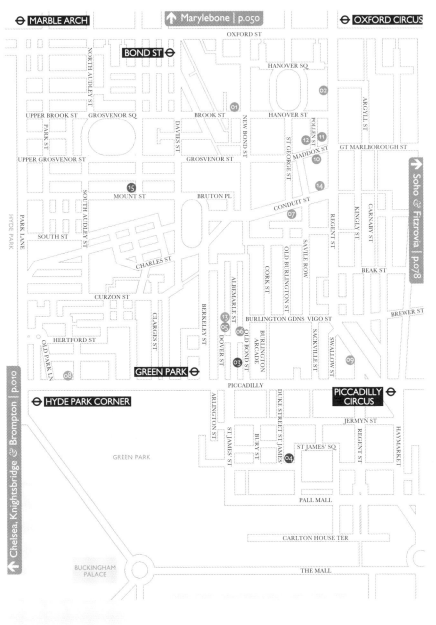

↑ Marylebone | p.050

→ Soho & Fitzrovia | p.078

← Chelsea, Knightsbridge & Brompton | p.010

MARBLE ARCH

OXFORD CIRCUS

BOND ST

GREEN PARK

HYDE PARK CORNER

PICCADILLY CIRCUS

OXFORD ST

HANOVER SQ

BROOK ST

HANOVER ST

NORTH AUDLEY ST

GROSVENOR SQ

UPPER BROOK ST

PARK ST

DAVIES ST

NEW BOND ST

POLLEN ST

ARGYLL ST

ST GEORGE ST

MADDOX ST

GT MARLBOROUGH ST

UPPER GROSVENOR ST

GROSVENOR ST

CONDUIT ST

SOUTH AUDLEY ST

MOUNT ST

BRUTON PL

REGENT ST

KINGLY ST

CARNABY ST

BEAK ST

HYDE PARK

PARK LANE

SOUTH ST

CHARLES ST

CURZON ST

SAVILE ROW

OLD BURLINGTON ST

CORK ST

ALBEMARLE ST

BREWER ST

HERTFORD ST

OLD PARK LN

CLARGES ST

BERKELEY ST

DOVER ST

OLD BOND ST

BURLINGTON GDNS VIGO ST

BURLINGTON ARCADE

SACKVILLE ST

SWALLOW ST

PICCADILLY

ARLINGTON ST

DUKE STREET ST JAMES

JERMYN ST

REGENT ST

HAYMARKET

ST JAMES' ST

BURY ST

ST JAMES

ST JAMES' SQ

GREEN PARK

PALL MALL

CARLTON HOUSE TER

BUCKINGHAM PALACE

THE MALL

● *Design galleries & institutions*

● *Design shops & C20th vintage*

● *Eat & drink (pp.072-073)*

01 ALESSI
02 APPLE STORE
03 CARPENTERS WORKSHOP GALLERY
04 DAVID GILL GALLERIES
05 DOVER STREET MARKET
06 PAUL SMITH NO 9

Street*wise*

When did you move to this street?
We moved to Mount Street in 2009. We had our first
tiny retail store on the corner of Manchester Square
and Duke Street and it was there that we discovered the
value of a great address without necessarily having the
largest or most prestigious shop. Sixteen years later, when
it became time to grow, we just walked in circles until we
reached Mount Street. This is it, we thought!

What originally attracted you to it?
The Mayfair address, the architecture, Scott's restaurant and it was
within walking distance of home – what more could we ask for?

**How has this shopping thoroughfare changed
since you've been here?**
Since we moved in, the street has completely changed. At the
time, Marc Jacobs had just opened along with Christian Louboutin,
and the rest were mostly antique shops and galleries. Of course,
there are some places which were and have remained destination
landmarks; the butcher Allens of Mayfair, menswear stores
Rubinacci and Hayward, Sautter Cigars, gunmakers William & Son.
Now pretty much every luxury brand is here or about to be here. And
since the refurbishment of The Connaught in 2007, it has become
not just a tourist but also a Londoner's retreat. Meanwhile, Mayfair
continues to be the new heart and soul of luxury London life.

What does the street offer the community that is unique?
It offers all the general services that you would expect – pubs,
clubs, a deli, restaurants, hunting and fishing supplies, a Porsche
dealership, as well as the oldest and best butcher in London.

Tell us about some of your neighbouring hotspots.
Scott's and 34 – whether you want steak or fish, these are two of
the finest restaurants of their kind in London; The Connaught bar;
Nicky Clarke, my hairdresser, and William & Son, my gunsmith.

**What has recently changed on neighbouring roads
that has alarmed you?**
Nothing alarms us. On the whole, due to the residential nature of
the whole neighbourhood, the only thing that has changed is the
retail which has gone from comatose to dynamic. Some people find
that alarming as part of the change but we find it to be a lifeline.

If you could change one thing on the street, what would it be?
The rent! I would defer my rent review.

Stephen Webster
Stephen Webster

93 MOUNT STREET W1K 2SY
0845 539 1840 STEPHENWEBSTER.COM

MOUNT STREET

01 ALESSI

22 BROOK STREET W1K 5DF
020 7518 9091
ALESSI.COM
MON–SAT 10–6:30, THU 10–7, SUN 12–6
BOND STREET

It did some of its most iconic work in the 1980s, when creative director Alberto Alessi hired pros like Michael Graves to design the famous post-modern hob kettle and Philippe Starck to draft the world's most iconic citrus juicer. Then, in the '90s, the company made a colourful statement with a whole raft of colourful and smiley accessories by the Milanese designer Stefano Giovannoni. Despite the playful appeal of those pieces, the look didn't travel so well into the new millennium, and it is Alessi's mission not to be defined by it.

Now nearly a century old, the company has had a new lease of life, hiring post-modernists like Pierre Charpin, Toyo Ito and Monica Förster to design kitchenware fresh enough to compete with 21st century successes. Staff at this London flagship, a triple-storey townhouse in a sea of shoe and fashion boutiques, are clearly excited by Förster's plain porcelain *Tower* measuring cups, and the new AlessiLux *Foreverlamp* LED lanterns, an energy-efficient twist on the paraffin lamp (both assistants I spoke to had one at home).

Alessi also moved quick to nab burgeoning stars from the Far East. Last year it collaborated with eight Chinese architects on a line of wood and stainless-steel serving pieces. And not a smiley face in sight.

02 APPLE STORE

235 REGENT STREET W1B 2EL
020 7153 9000
APPLE.COM
MON–SAT 9–9, SUN 12–6
OXFORD CIRCUS

Apple has been at the forefront of the wired world, ever improving on its own highly usable products to the point that we can be everywhere while nowhere in particular. And yet here on Regent Street and in the Apple Stores that have followed worldwide, it has designed one of the most successful face-to-face experiences in retail. There are few Grade II-listed buildings, in London or elsewhere, that can boast queues of tech-savvy youth waiting every morning for the doors to open. But this location has managed to preserve a priceless mosaic façade while retrofitting an interior that can support such crowds with elbow room to spare.

This could've been the kind of place to frustrate even informed consumers to tears, yet Apple staffers are helpful, experienced, honest and, most importantly, ubiquitous. They'll let you test the heck out of the equipment, even if they know you're bound to leave empty handed. This longtime Apple user was especially sceptical of the Genius Bar, a free service for customers having technical issues. But it's easy to get same-day service, provided you book online before opening hours. Can Dell say as much?

CARPENTERS WORKSHOP GALLERY

3 ALBEMARLE STREET W1S 4HE

020 3051 5939

CARPENTERSWORKSHOPGALLERY.COM

MON-FRI 10-6

GREEN PARK

Its Mayfair address is just as swellegant as the big-name art dealers, but there's something different about Carpenters Workshop Gallery. One of London's first forums for collectible design, it can compete piece for piece with the most avant-garde artists in quality, concept and resonance. And yet everything shown in this pared-back, slick-surfaced space can be classified as furniture and should be used, albeit with care. The name 'functional sculpture' doesn't quite do it justice.

Loic Le Gaillard and Julien Lombrail began their outfit a decade ago in, unsurprisingly, a carpenter's workshop. But it took little time for the founders to be recognised for their singular eye for talent and undisputable good taste: the Moooi favourite Maarten Baas was an early contributor, as was mad Dutch collective Atelier Van Lieshout. They outgrew that Chelsea space in a few years and expanded into works by Random International, Nendo and Andrea Branzi on Albemarle Street – and, last year, an industrial space back home in Paris. The former can seem antiseptic, a bit lonely, while you contemplate the message of works like Branzi's anthropological birch furniture (pictured). Yet the ambition of this design rightfully needs space to breathe and expand.

DAVID GILL GALLERIES
2-4 KING STREET SW1Y 6QP
020 3195 6600
DAVIDGILLGALLERIES.COM
MON–FRI 10-6, SAT 11-6
GREEN PARK

To enter David Gill is to leave one century and enter another leagues ahead. It takes up a swathe of first-class real estate next to the august Christie's auction house, between gracious Piccadilly and the Georgian St James's Square, but the former solicitors' office has been opened up with a series of immense vertical windows, vaulted ceilings and polished-concrete floors. And it's furnished with a vision of the future crafted by designers at the absolute bleeding edge.

Gill is one of the reasons auction houses like Christie's have embraced design as a high-art form. The Spanish veteran cut his teeth showing Europeans like Eileen Gray and Charlotte Perriand in the 1980s before adopting indefatigable Brits like Ron Arad. He made stars of surrealist designers Fredrikson Stallard and was instrumental in adding 'furniture designer' to architect Zaha Hadid's repertoire – indeed, he launched this space with her *Liquid Glacial* tables, like melting shards of ice suspended in time.

Slick, deceptive surfaces are a running theme here. Gaetano Pesce's *Six Tables on Water* were like functional oil slicks. And recently, gallery-goers thrilled to see Barnaby Barford's mirrors, framed by clusters of ceramic flowers that on closer inspection exemplified the seven deadly sins – there being only seven, the attendant was delighted to steer us through each one.

05 DOVER STREET MARKET
- 17-18 DOVER STREET W1S 4LT
- 020 7518 0680
- DOVERSTREETMARKET.COM
- MON–WED 11-6:30, THU–SAT 11-7, SUN 12-5
- GREEN PARK

It is, at its heart, a fashion retailer, as devastatingly avant-garde as it is exclusive. A concept shop of entirely original concept, it exhibits a tightly curated selection of designer wear governed by the meticulous eye of Comme des Garçons' Rei Kawakubo. Incidentally, less than half of the content is Comme and, as it turns out, Kawakubo has devised a brilliant formula; DSM is still thriving nearly a decade after launching in this eponymous Mayfair street, and last year a Tokyo location was added.

But interior design and architecture aficionados love it here, too. For starters, the fashion – not only by Comme but also structure junkies like Alaïa, Chalayan and Thom Browne – is built to be admired from all angles. The real treat, though, is the *tachiagari*, the biannual 'new beginning' that sees the space redesigned throughout its intimate showspaces. Within each department, market 'stalls' are rebuilt (in decidedly ramshackle materials like corrugated metal, salvaged wood and real scaffolding), surreal sculpture casts shadows over £500 T-shirts, and exciting seating appears for patient partners in wait.

06 PAUL SMITH NO 9
- 9 ALBEMARLE STREET W1S 4HH
- 020 7493 4565
- PAULSMITH.CO.UK
- MON–SAT 10:30-6, THU 10:30-7
- GREEN PARK

For a designer who brings in hundreds of millions a year from dedicated shops in 30 countries, Paul Smith has an uncommon fascination with independent design. A man with a respect for handiwork, who often appears personally in his Notting Hill shop to pin hems, he collects bits and bobs from his travels, venturing off-piste from the fashion-retail centres in Tokyo, Moscow and Mumbai to sniff out specimens of fine craftsmanship that stand the test of our discerning times.

This boutique has doubled as a gallery for a curated collection of these pieces since it opened in 2005. But fashion eventually horned in on the space and, in 2013, it closed for an expansion into Stafford Street. Our press time preceded the unveiling, though we're told the featured design will embody the same Paul Smith brand of panache and good fun that the previous shop was known for. It'll make room for items of 'furniture, objects and curiosities' touched by the designer himself – in the past he's collaborated on footballs and sideboards, tea sets and bike saddles, and reupholstered vintage finds with his own zippy fabrics – but will also introduce decoration by artists from the legendary to the unknown. An exciting development in a freshly relevant Mayfair.

07 *Classic French dining*

Much loved French chef Eric Chavot makes his return to London in the Westbury Hotel. Chandelier-clad room with red leather upholstery and stunning mosaic floor throughout.

BRASSERIE CHAVOT 41 CONDUIT STREET W1S 2YF

020 7183 6425 | BRASSERIECHAVOT.COM

08 *South American vibe*

Peruvian-style restaurant and bar with terracotta tiled floor, colourful interior and South American spirit. Ceviche Bar, open charcoal grill from the central kitchen. Pisco Bar focuses on piscos, rums and tequilas. Good live music programme.

COYA 118 PICCADILLY W1J 7NW

020 7042 7118 | COYARESTAURANT.COM

09 *Fish in a steak restaurant*

Sumptuous green leather booths and armchairs, parquet flooring in this long curved room overlooking Regent Street. Latest Hawksmoor venue has teamed up with top seafood chef Mitch Tonks to offer fish, as well as some of the best steak in London.

HAWKSMOOR AIR STREET [PICTURED] 58 AIR STREET W1J 0AD

020 7406 3980 | THEHAWKSMOOR.COM/AIRSTREET

10 *Michelin bargain lunch*

Refined, exquisite cooking from chef-patron Claude Bosi. Go at lunch to experience a two Michelin-starred restaurant. Wooden floor, subdued colours, linen and attentive service make this a Mayfair must.

HIBISCUS 29 MADDOX STREET W1S 2PA

020 7629 2999 | HIBISCUSRESTAURANT.CO.UK

11 *Dinner hideaway*

Jason Atherton's second restaurant across the street from original. This is a dark, hideaway bistro. Ox-blood banquettes, hardwood chairs, antique tables, and distressed walls. Don't leave before you've had the *tarte tatin* for two.

LITTLE SOCIAL 5 POLLEN STREET W1S 1NE
020 7870 3730 | LITTLESOCIAL.CO.UK

12 *Refined flavours*

Masterful cooking from chef Jason Atherton, professionally served in elegant, light-filled setting. Popular for its original and elaborate flavour combinations and presentation. Culinary gem.

POLLEN STREET SOCIAL 8-10 POLLEN STREET W1S 1NQ
020 7290 7600 | POLLENSTREETSOCIAL.COM

13 *Fashionable tea and cake*

Rose Carrarini opened her bakery and cafe on the top floor of the fashion haven that is DSM in 2007. Minimal space with communal tables. Friendly staff serve homemade quiches, breads, salads and delicious carrot cake and brownies.

ROSE'S AT DOVER STREET MARKET 17-18 DOVER ST W1S 4LT
020 7518 0680 | LONDON.DOVERSTREETMARKET.COM

14 *Champagne afternoon tea*

Multi-room Mayfair house offers extravagant dining experience at the Lecture Room and cosy afternoon tea at the Parlour. Artists alter the interior to the Gallery restaurant, and the Glade is more woodland than bar. Check out the toilets. Open late.

SKETCH 9 CONDUIT STREET W1S 2XG
020 7659 4500 | SKETCH.UK.COM

Place to sleep? 15

THE CONNAUGHT HOTEL THE-CONNAUGHT.CO.UK

PREMISES, RENTS & RATES *continued from p.063*

MAGNUS ENGLUND

For us, a typical rent hike has been 50%, even
though we have a very good negotiator, we
call him the bulldog and he does quite a
good job for us!

MAX FRASER

But you're the ones who have made the area
more upmarket. It doesn't seem fair.

LINA KANAFANI

That is how it works. They invite you
to come in at a good rent because
you have a good image and they like
your work. After three to five years,
other larger companies are attracted
who can afford much more and the
rent then doubles or triples.

SHERIDAN COAKLEY

But it's all swings and roundabouts. In
theory that brings in more trade, which
means you should do more business. The
converse is that you move somewhere else,
where the rent matches the kind of business
that you want to do. There are quite a lot
of spaces in London to choose from.

RHONDA DRAKEFORD

We're quite lucky in that our whole street is
owned by the same landlord so our rent is
level with everybody else. If they change one,
everybody knows about it and you kind of fight
for each other. It is a rare situation.

SHERIDAN COAKLEY

Rent is about as reasonable a system as you
are ever going to get. It reflects what kind
of market it is. Tracey, you're on Redchurch
Street, which is changing phenomenally
week by week. You'll probably have to make
a decision at some point in the near future
as to whether your turnover has increased
enough to afford the rent being generated
from the other trade that is coming in.

TRACEY NEULS

Yeah, I mean a lot of it is the media hype that

is around Redchurch Street right now, helping to artificially hike the rent. Yes, maybe the odd tourist comes by, but such hype doesn't necessarily translate into significant people coming in off the street.

SHERIDAN COAKLEY

I don't think it's the landlords but the opportunistic brands. A lot of them can't justify their turnover on the street, but they just want to be on that street. That is more damaging than what the landlords are doing.

TRACEY NEULS

On the one hand there are the rents. And yes, the influx from other brands, too. When I arrived, I went up against a major French brand that was not aligned to the ethos of the street. In reality, it might be the rent hikes that push me out, but it is also probably going to be the neighbours, and I think that is a little bit sad, too.

MAGNUS ENGLUND

I have never seen an area develop so quickly. Aren't Marc Jacobs and Prada the latest ones to have signed up for Redchurch Street?

TRACEY NEULS

I've been there a year and a half and I haven't seen any of them. Following the hype and the false claims from the press, a burn out could be possible because there is nothing to back it up. At the moment, you walk down Redchurch Street and there are spaces to rent so where are the people who are supposedly moving in?

MAX FRASER

Ok, let's talk about business rates. Regardless of whether you own or rent, what proportion of your outgoings do rates represent?

SHERIDAN COAKLEY

It's about 45% of the rental value, which is pretty accurate these days.

SIMON ALDERSON

Like rent, it's also calculated according to the size of your shop frontage, so will be higher if you have an enormous frontage compared to a narrow, deep shop.

MAX FRASER

Justin, your motivation for these sizeable premises here in Clerkenwell are slightly different from the others in the room.

Continued p.090

HEAL'S

Furnishing the best homes since 1810

Soho & Fitzrovia

078

● Design galleries & institutions
● Design shops & C20th vintage

● Eat & drink (pp.088-089)

01 19 GREEK STREET
02 THE BUILDING CENTRE
03 EDC LONDON
04 FRITZ HANSEN, REPUBLIC OF
05 GALLERY LIBBY SELLERS
06 HABITAT
07 HEAL'S
08 LIBERTY
09 LIGNE ROSET WEST END

10 MINOTTI LONDON
11 MUJI (p.102)

Street*wise*

When did you move to this street?
We moved to Great Titchfield Street in 2009, although my wife had been working in the area since the year before.

What particularly attracted you to it?
The high demographic of media, fashion, design and advertising people. The proximity to Oxford Street and the opportunity to create a business that was more of a match to the local clientele than what was already on offer.

How has the surrounding area changed since you've been here?
Our coffee shop Kaffeine brings over 3,000 people a week to our little section of Great Titchfield Street and our long term workers and residents say that Kaffeine has helped to change the area into a neighbourhood that is much more enticing, welcoming, modern and community focussed. More people are now aware of Great Titchfield Street as a village of central London that still has more potential to develop.

What does the street offer the community that is unique?
The street is quiet, safe, friendly, hospitable and clean, and there is a good mix of independent shops, restaurants and pubs.

Tell us about some of your neighbouring hotspots.
Riding House Café at all times… The Crown & Sceptre pub on a sunny afternoon… and The Green Man pub (in Riding House Street) for cider.

If you could change one thing on the street, what would it be?
Fitzrovia has been donated over 500 trees through a community group on Portland Place, but the only street in the area not to receive them has been Great Titchfield Street. We would like to see more trees planted in our area.

Peter Dore-Smith
Kaffeine

66 GREAT TITCHFIELD STREET W1W 7OJ
020 7580 6755 KAFFEINE.CO.UK

GREAT TITCHFIELD ST

01 19 GREEK STREET

19 GREEK STREET W1D 4DT
020 7734 5594
19GREEKSTREET.COM
MON–SAT 10–6, SUN 12–6
TOTTENHAM COURT ROAD

This very tall, very narrow Soho townhouse uses every square metre of its six storeys – and the welcoming staff will insist, after buzzing you in, that you begin at the very top. It's a decent strategy: creative director Marc Péridis provides a home to the Brazilian contemporary design collective Espasso and Australian environmental designers Supercyclers, but its own commissioned pieces are at the top.

A self-trained and successful interior designer with his own practice, Montage, Péridis has a natural eye for furniture with fresh shapes and materials and an emphasis on craft. His latest top-floor residents include a range of straight-back sorbet-hued chairs developed with Nina Tolstrup of Studiomama and exhibited during Milan's Salone del Mobile 2013 at the Marc by Marc Jacobs boutique. And one floor below, Tel Aviv designers Noam Dover and Michal Cederbaum have charged traditional Middle Eastern materials with new applications, like their series of limited-edition spun-steel tables constructed from 'saj' domes, originally used for making pita bread.

The international make-up of the offering creates a variety not often seen in curated spaces. The juxtaposition is especially evident on the non-commercial basement level, where Péridis arranges 'social-impact' pieces in all matter of materials and scales.

02 THE BUILDING CENTRE

- 🏪 STORE STREET WC1E 7BT
- 📞 020 7692 4000
- ➤ BUILDINGCENTRE.CO.UK
- 🕐 MON-FRI 9:30-6, SAT 10-5
- ⊖ GOODGE STREET

I can't count the number of times I've walked right past The Building Centre – wondering what it had done to deserve such incredible real estate, housed as it is in this beautiful building at an unusual dip in the road. Quite a lot, it turns out. This builders' resource centre, in operation for more than 80 years, keeps track of the city's built developments and offers advice, information and support to the industry. It also houses New London Architecture, a sort of think tank that sponsors debates and lectures about the industry.

Yet for the layperson there is much about the centre to love, as you'll see if you resolve, like me, to finally enter it and see. A scale model of central London, for instance, constantly evolving with colossal developments like the Shard, as well as reimagined parks and transport bridges. Galleries scattered around the ground floor exhibit new-fangled building materials, products and energy-savers, but the focus is on the main gallery, which displays artistic architectural interpretations of the future of building. There's also a RIBA-sponsored bookshop, accessed at the rear, offering titles relating to home building, renovation and design.

03 EDC LONDON

- 🏪 20 MARGARET STREET W1W 8RS
- 📞 020 7631 1090
- ➤ EDCLONDON.COM
- 🕐 MON-SAT 10-6
- ⊖ OXFORD CIRCUS

If you had cherry-picked the most luxurious, sophisticated pieces from the finest contemporary brands on the continent, and found an exclusive central London townhouse in which to arrange them, you would probably shout it from the rooftops. The 200-square-metre European Design Centre showroom prefers to remain the introverted sister to Minotti down the road (p.087). A darling of the trade operating in London's more polished neighbourhoods, EDC quietly welcomes decorators and their clients to a showroom set up rather as a refined city home, all parquet floors, flamboyant wallpaper and warm, tailored upholstery – and established names from Knoll and Foscarini to Casamilano.

Its understated character could also be its downfall, alas. EDC has moved its entrance from street level to an awkward garden-level door accessed by a slick iron stairwell. And this must discourage visitors, because as I entered recently, the entire workforce were nestled into a suede-covered *S-Perla* sofa by Henge – an irresistible piece, to be fair. Having spoiled their morning *kaffeeklatsch*, I couldn't shake the feeling I was trespassing on the home of the grande dame. And the servants weren't happy about it.

04 FRITZ HANSEN, REPUBLIC OF

13 MARGARET STREET W1W 8RN

020 7637 5534

FRITZHANSEN.COM

MON-SAT 10-6:30, THU 10-7, SUN 10-5

OXFORD CIRCUS

Now this is how a retail flagship should be. Even in London's historic heart, where the response to all building permits is 'no', Fritz Hansen has managed to carve out a veritable republic of a space: deep, vast and spacious, punctuated with tableaux of handsome, useful objects.

The Danish brand teamed up with like-minded crowd-pleaser Skandium to launch this Scandinavian extravaganza a few years ago, working with the homewares purveyor to put its furnishings in a homely context. So you'll get the Arne Jacobsen oeuvre – the iconic *Ant, Series 7, Swan* and *Egg* chairs – and the range of timeless Poul Kjaerholm tables, delightfully propped with *Kaiser Idell Luxus* lamps by Christian Dell, Louis Poulsen lights and mischievous wooden toys such as giant Rosendahl monkeys. Shop assistants seem to take their cues from the monkeys – swinging towards you with a smile to help you track down a white version of Kasper Salto's *Little Friend* table or explain the provenance of that gold bicycle on display by the till.

This area of London, that of Fitzrovia, is on a mission to establish itself as a design hub of London through the formation of the Fitzrovia Now initiative, comprising a coterie of like-minded design retailers and showrooms. The Republic of Fritz Hansen sits firmly at its centre.

05 GALLERY LIBBY SELLERS

41-42 BERNERS STREET W1T 3NB

020 3384 8785

LIBBYSELLERS.COM

TUE-FRI 11-6

GOODGE STREET

Back when only the auction houses were showing and selling collectible design, Libby Sellers – one-time curator at the Design Museum – saw a future in it. She engaged young, talented designers, some still studying at schools across Europe, and encouraged thoughtful, limited-edition works, which she supported at pop-up exhibitions across London and beyond.

Discoveries like Nicolas Le Moigne, Moritz Waldemeyer and Julia Lohmann emerged into stars under Sellers' wing, using unusual materials or processes to comment on politics, history, even pop culture. As a result, interest in collectible design grew, and Sellers was able to invest in this gallery, a quiet, flood-lit space in Fitzrovia. The modest front room is just big enough for exhibiting a simple, tightly curated idea; the recent *8 Chairs*, for instance, by London duo Clarke & Reilly, was exactly that – an opportunity to view eight remarkable chairs from all angles and, in the viewing, learn of their complex history. A smaller room, used for experimental pieces, is similarly washed with natural light.

Libby is often present, popping out of the back office with a smile and more than happy to explain the often layered raison d'être behind the talents on display, talking up tomorrow's collectibles at the cusp.

06 HABITAT

- 196-199 TOTTENHAM COURT ROAD W1T 7PJ
- 0844 499 1122
- HABITAT.CO.UK
- MON-SAT 10-7, THU 10-8, SUN 12-6
- GOODGE STREET

As the previous edition of this guide went to press, Habitat had put all but three of its 33 UK stores into administration. The brand was picked up by Home Retail Group, owner of Argos and Homebase. And a nation wept for the unfeasibly low-priced homewares that were also incomparably well designed.

Habitat was one of the few retailers that would get accolades in the spectrum of design press. None of its Tottenham Court Road peers have half its charisma. And yet now we are down to three locations: King's Road, Finchley Road and this TCR flagship.

In the couple of years since the London implosion, the company has managed to pull its socks up and stay the course, but not much more. Rather than drafting a business model embracing something closer to the big-box culture at Homebase, it has continued on with its trendy palettes, delicious linens, adorable bedsit sofas and modular storage. But gone are the high-profile designer collaborations (a shrewd move, perhaps), and crowd-pleasers like Tord Boontje's *Garland* lamps.

Habitat was founded on the radical entrepreneurial vision of Terence Conran in 1964. At a time when retail can't afford to coast along, it's a shame Habitat can't pull its socks up faster and embrace the verve lying in its very foundations.

07 HEAL'S

🚩 196 TOTTENHAM COURT ROAD W1T 7LQ

📞 020 7636 1666

↖ HEALS.CO.UK

🕐 MON-WED, FRI 10-7, THU 10-8, SUN 12-6

⊖ GOODGE STREET

At more than 200 years old, it is the *éminence grise* of Tottenham Court Road's design community, but in 2013, acknowledging that there is no space for complacency in retail today, Heal's went to great efforts to enhance its flagship, streamline the product selection and overhaul its merchandising, giving Heal's the more upmarket vibe it deserves.

A lot of attention has been lavished on the prominent window displays and main entrance foyer gallery, where seasonal or coherently themed storytelling occurs. On my last visit, it had been turfed with artificial grass and was laden with plants, complete with greenhouse and iconic caravan as props. I made my way upstairs for a coffee in the Tom Dixon-designed Heal's Quarter Cafe before test driving the extensive furniture choices on this floor. Check out the designer collaborations while you're here – the Heal's Discovers range is a safe way into well-priced design by Young Turks like Lee Broom, Jake Phipps, Katie Walker and John Galvin. On the second floor, it has returned to its mattress-making roots with the Heal's Sleep Studio where you can get sound advice for a sound night's sleep.

The changes at Heal's have been courageous and should be supported. I just hope that it can hold its nerve and maintain its new trading principles in a rather jittery retail market.

08 LIBERTY
REGENT STREET W1B 5AH
020 7734 1234
LIBERTY.CO.UK
MON-SAT 10-8, SUN 12-6
OXFORD CIRCUS

The British design explosion of the Noughties could have passed Liberty by, it of the Tudor revival building and the back catalogue of conservative cotton florals. But a decade ago the company resolved to update its trove of European and Asian antiques. It still keeps a rich cache of Art Deco loungers, Indian baby chairs and vintage pantry cupboards (with provenance that any number of assistants would thrill to share), but now it offers contemporary seating from Case and Vitra, dining furniture by Tom Dixon and De Padova and the Danish company Hay. Then, in 2011, it opened a concession for the online home and garden shop Re-found Objects, expanding its outdoor living department into a force not only pensioners can appreciate.

Take the lift to the fourth floor and follow the progression from contemporary to antique to garden to lighting, where Lee Broom's brilliant crystal bulbs hang beautifully against the dark wood panelling. The shop is built around a wonderful central atrium that brings energy up from the lower floors, and there are discreet staircases here and there to lead you into departments you wouldn't normally visit, like the haberdashery, where a sales associate spends her quiet moments knitting.

09 LIGNE ROSET WEST END
23-25 MORTIMER STREET W1T 3JE
020 7323 1248
LIGNE-ROSET-WESTEND.CO.UK
MON-SAT 10-6, THU 10-8, SUN 12-5
GOODGE STREET

Across the road is a massive hole in the ground where the old Middlesex Hospital used to be and where the apartments of Fitzroy Place will soon overlook Ligne Roset's central-London showroom. These days all that machinery is an annoyance, not least to LR's stoical staff. Still, it's not all bad news, they remind me: the residents of Fitzroy will provide a built-in market for this purveyor of aspirational urban furnishings.

If they're anything like me, they won't be able to resist the scene through the double-height glass windows. An upside-down version of the brand's City location (p.153), LR West End extends over the main and basement levels of this comparatively petite space. As such, the collection on show is highly edited, showing only the latest ranges in the most covetable new colours – like the inimitable *Felt* chair designed by Delo Lindo. With one exception. The company recently celebrated the 40th birthday of its iconic *Togo* sofa, designed by Michel Ducaroy. So the *Togo* gets the front-and-centre treatment these days, in new candy-coloured upholstery treatments. It still seems as fresh as it was when it and I were in our youth – and not at all upstaged by the brand's new guard.

10 MINOTTI LONDON

77 MARGARET STREET W1W 8SY

020 7323 3233

MINOTTILONDON.COM

MON-FRI 9:30-6, SAT 10-6

OXFORD CIRCUS

It's impossible not to feel shabby walking into Minotti's magnificent London headquarters, the raised-ground floor of an equally polished heritage mansion block at the tasteful end of Fitzrovia – particularly against the staff, all immaculately turned out in the Milanese way. Happily, they can see past that, greeting you as they might a keen investor. The company has been putting out well-crafted, modern, five-star-hotel luxury for more than 60 years, and the enduring attention to detail extends to old-fashioned hospitality.

The five-year-old showroom was a genius move by the company, which works in partnership with EDC nearby (p.081); it allows visitors to inspect the fine detail in the finishes and upholsteries, subtle features that are impossible to pick up online. Each deep, plush sofa is like an expensive piece of Italian couture, tailored in suiting and nubbly wools. Minotti didn't get the memo that white was out – they wrote the memo, offering instead a palette of moody greys, raspberries, purples and browns – eyeshadow colours – plus rich-grained walnut cabinets and metallics that need polishing twice a day. The staff, naturally, doesn't see anything wrong with the level of upkeep necessary for a brass drinks table. The Minotti lifestyle is ideally suited to them.

12 *The perfect lunch*

Modest restaurant in heart of Soho serving superb, simple, small dishes. Daily changing menu focuses on Brit and European produce. Book for lunch but no reservations for dinner so expect to queue.

10 GREEK STREET 10 GREEK STREET W1D 4DH
020 7734 4677 | 10GREEKSTREET.COM

13 *Sandwich in a toilet*

Converted Victorian underground toilet has been lovingly transformed into a café serving Caravan coffee, pastries, daily changing sandwiches, soups and salads. Sit at the original porcelain urinals to enjoy a cuppa.

THE ATTENDANT 27A FOLEY STREET W1W 6DY
020 7637 3794 | THE-ATTENDANT.COM

14 *Go experimental*

Exciting cooking from a young chef destined for greatness. Lunch is a bargain, four courses for £28, but it's tricky to get a table. Head to Oskar's Bar and wait until one is free. Industrial feel throughout.

DABBOUS 39 WHITFIELD STREET W1T 2SF
020 7323 1544 | DABBOUS.CO.UK

15 *Coffee and toastie*

Deli, charcuterie and cheese room. Sister wine bar around the corner at 43 Lexington Street. Espresso bar a few streets away on St Anne's Court. Fresh quality produce make the Spanish-style sandwiches a must. Cakes and pastries, too.

FERNANDEZ & WELLS 73 BEAK STREET W1F 9SR
020 7287 8124 | FERNANDEZANDWELLS.COM

16 *Tapas & sherry*

This restaurant and sherry bar may be 10 years old, but its contemporary tapas are some of the best in London. Wash down with a fine selection of sherries. Sister restaurant Barrafina is on Dean Street, Catalonian tapas bar.

FINO 33 CHARLOTTE STREET (ENTRANCE ON RATHBONE ST)
W1T 1RR | 020 7813 8010 | FINORESTAURANT.COM

17 *Authentic noodles*

Small, stripped back canteen. Affordable Japanese serving noodles (in particular, udon noodles), soups, tempura and some rice dishes. A favourite amongst London's top chefs.

KOYA 49 FRITH STREET W1D 4SG

020 7434 4463 | KOYA.CO.UK

18 *British cooking at its best*

Tavern downstairs is informal, extensive wine list and British seafood selection. Upstairs dining room is full of reclaimed Georgian furniture with images of Brit landscape, seafood and produce from their suppliers throughout. Menu changes daily.

NEWMAN STREET TAVERN [PICTURED] 48 NEWMAN ST W1T 1QQ

020 3667 1445 | NEWMANSTREETTAVERN.CO.UK

19 *Sunny flavours*

From Ottolenghi founders, Nopi offers Med-Middle Eastern-Asian flavours cleverly combined. Open for breakfast, lunch and dinner, cocktails and food served at the bar too. White interior with marble and brass details.

NOPI 21-22 WARWICK STREET W1B 5NE

020 7494 9584 | NOPI-RESTAURANT.COM

20 *Italian pastries & cakes*

Authentic Italian bakery-turned-canteen designed by Claudio Silvestrin; stone floors, bronze fittings and one long narrow communal table. Mouth-watering display of pastries, cakes, breads and pizzas. Buzzing morning to night.

PRINCI 135 WARDOUR STREET W1F 0UT

020 7478 8888 | PRINCI.CO.UK

21 *Underground cocktails*

Space is 'just as Rev JW Simpson left it', apparently; woodchip, pastel tiles, crumbly walls but with new retro-style furniture. It's all about the cocktails – flips, sours and fizzes.

REVEREND JW SIMPSON 33 GOODGE STREET W1T 2QJ

020 3174 1155 | REVJWSIMPSON.COM

Place to sleep? 22

DEAN STREET TOWNHOUSE DEANSTREETTOWNHOUSE.COM

PREMISES, RENTS & RATES *continued from p. 075*

I suppose you could argue that the Knoll showroom is an advert for Knoll as a global brand?

JUSTIN PRATT

It is, but our rents and rates are split over a number of different businesses. It is quite a small percentage generally of the whole business and so is not a daily threat to us.

MAX FRASER

Does it help to have other like-minded retailers in your area?

SHERIDAN COAKLEY

I wish we had more. I think it generates more business and it's very convenient for people.

LINA KANAFANI

An area becomes a destination and more interesting as a result. You don't want to go to a street with only one shop – you want to go somewhere with four shops.

MAX FRASER

And what about gentrification? Is it just an inevitability that big chains will move in off the back of the independent retailers making a street interesting?

SHERIDAN COAKLEY

I don't think it's an issue. Either you survive in that area or if it becomes unstoppable with major brands then you just have to move and it's not the end of the world. What we do is quite niche, and a lot of it is destination-driven so people will seek us out.

RHONDA DRAKEFORD

I guess you have to hope that you would gain some new customers even if you might lose some, too.

SIMON ALDERSON

I think you would have to respond to your locality and adjust and adapt to the customer.

LINA KANAFANI

When my shop moved from Marylebone to Brompton, I had to undergo a total change. It took three years and I had to change the business totally.

MAX FRASER

And Neil, as an analyst working with large retailers, what is their attitude to up-and-coming areas?

NEIL SAUNDERS

Certainly the bigger retailers are very focussed on the up-and-coming areas because they

are desperate for footfall and desperate for people to spend, and they will move to the locations that provide those things, which are often the ones which are in fact unique and interesting. They meet resistance from locals, but if they can afford the rent there is nothing that residents can do to stop them moving in. And when they do move in, those protesting residents start to use them anyway.

STORYTELLING

MAX FRASER
I'm interested in this idea that some of you might call yourself curators, not just retailers. Is your role about editing out choice rather than providing heaps of it?

RHONDA DRAKEFORD
Definitely for us.

The curation and the way that we put things together, and the experience of walking around the space is key to our message

LINA KANAFANI
It depends what you do and your size. Like Darkroom and myself, personality is what we would rely on. I think for some of the bigger stores, you would rely on something different and wouldn't focus just on personality but a certain core of products.

SIMON ALDERSON
It isn't only about the product, whichever way you present it. You have to consider if it's going to work for your customer base. How you present it is part of the story telling, together with the way the service is run and the way that people receive the goods.

RHONDA DRAKEFORD
I think a lot of what we all do is choose products with a story. The way it looks is also very important, but talking someone through a product is often what clinches the sale.

TRACEY NEULS
What I find is that you can visit any department store, purchase something and leave the shop and you've never once spoken to or made eye contact with somebody.

Continued p.106

London's leading design destination

designjunction

London / Milan / New York
thedesignjunction.co.uk

Covent Garden & Holborn

W.C.1

W.C.2

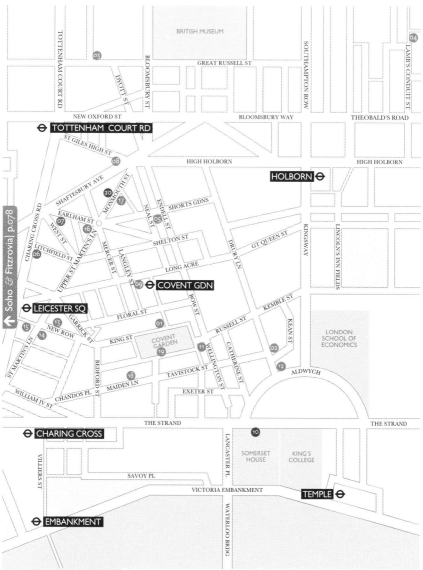

← Soho & Fitzrovia p.078

Design galleries & institutions
Design shops & C20th vintage
Design bookshops

Eat & drink (pp.104-105)

01 APPLE STORE *(p.068)*
02 ARAM
03 ARTEMIDE
04 DARKROOM
05 DO
06 KOENIG BOOKS
07 MAGMA
08 MOLTENI&C DADA
09 MUJI
10 SOMERSET HOUSE

Street*wise*

When did you move to this street?
December 2009.

What particularly attracted you to it?
Lamb's Conduit Street was a big catalyst in making Darkroom the
shop it has become. My business partner Rhonda Drakeford and
I were familiar with the street, but it wasn't until we cycled past an
empty location on it that we started to consider it as a possible
option for our shop. We decided it was ideal because of its unique
nature – the whole street is owned by one of England's oldest
private schools, Rugby, and has been for several hundred years.
They have a policy of only renting spaces to independent retailers
and are careful not to allow too many crossovers in terms of stock.

How has the area changed since you've been here?
The area has become more popular in the time we've been here,
both from the point of view of retailers wishing to move here, as well
as general footfall. There has also been a spurt of men's clothing
stores opening, which has bought a younger weekend crowd.

What does the street offer the community that is unique?
The fact that the street only houses independent retailers is
itself unique in London. There is a fascinating mix of old and new
boutiques, restaurants, cafes, tailors and even London's oldest
funeral parlour (which incidentally buried Lord Nelson!).

Tell us about some of your neighbouring hotspots.
The Espresso Room is a tiny coffee bar serving the best coffee in
Bloomsbury – if not London! Folk Ladies sells casual clothing and
footwear, as well as other designers such as Acné, and they also
stock Aesop beauty products. Ben Pentreath for its unusual mix
of gifts and things for the home, and Persephone Books, which
reprints neglected classics by (mostly women) writers.

What has recently changed that has alarmed you?
The closure of the only chain, Starbucks, was a big surprise, but
hopefully means a change in people's habits as The Espresso Room
on the neighbouring street has a thriving business.

If you could change one thing on the street, what would it be?
The popularity of the street has definitely grown in the time we've
been here, but it still lacks a certain amount of footfall. The general
awareness of Lamb's Conduit Street is relatively niche and as a
community we need to work harder to raise the profile of the area
as a whole, as once customers find us they're always converted!

Lulu Roper-Caldbeck
Darkroom

52 LAMB'S CONDUIT STREET WC1N 3LL
020 7831 7244 DARKROOMLONDON.COM

LAMB'S CONDUIT ST

02 ARAM
110 DRURY LANE WC2B 5SG
020 7557 7557
ARAM.CO.UK
MON-SAT 10-6, THU 10-7
COVENT GARDEN

This Drury Lane emporium may be the only Aram most people have ever known, but in fact Aram has been synonymous with contemporary lifestyle since before there was such a thing. It took Zeev Aram – a design graduate who apprenticed with Erno Goldfinger – to convince London there was a modern alternative to Chippendale. His first space on the King's Road, acquired in the mid-1960s, distributed designs by Le Corbusier, Charlotte Perriand and Castiglioni that were so foreign to these parts as to be shocking. But they sold. Zeev himself would contribute to the modernist canon with his *Dino* storage system and *Altra* tables, before looking to the US for contributions from Herman Miller and Eames. He was one of the first champions of modernist pioneer Eileen Gray.

Gray's work, for which Aram holds the worldwide licence, is still a bestseller at Drury Lane, run by an effortlessly knowledgeable team. The 1,800-square-metre industrial space pays as much heed to the designers who helped build the company as to heavy-hitting manufacturers like USM, Tecta and Arper. In this location they've assembled as comprehensive a collection as anything you'll find in town – if you're hunting for storage, there are a dozen wall units that can play to your specs, and if you're into lighting, this is your proverbial one-stop shop. Be sure to check out the rolling programme of contemporary exhibitions on the top floor.

03 ARTEMIDE

106 GREAT RUSSELL STREET WC1B 3NB

020 7291 3853

ARTEMIDE.COM

MON–SAT 9–5 (CLOSED FOR LUNCH 1–1.30)

TOTTENHAM COURT ROAD

Those clogging up Tottenham Court Road would be hard-pressed to track you down at this pleasant Bloomsbury townhouse; only shoppers with a purpose ever make it here. But those folks are missing out – on a modest yet lively space that will cure your SAD and a quiet corner to discover lighting solutions that could well change your life.

Put chandeliers out of your mind for now. Artemide has been in the business of simple, bare-bones lighting since 1960, when it was founded in Italy by Ernesto Gismondi. He attracted the leading lights of the industry to design not just wow-factor installations for retailers and hoteliers, but accessible practical solutions for the home. The latter is what this boutique is about: the *Calenda* suspension lights by Italo Rota and Alessandro Pedretti, perfect for a hallway or kitchen; the blobby *Castore* family by Michele De Lucchi and Huub Ubbens; and Vico Magistretti's retro-futuristic desk lamps. You could easily walk away with a *Tolomeo Pinza* clip lamp by De Lucchi, as I once did. Just unclip one of the new coloured versions from the display table and go – it's the most reliable piece of Italian design you'll get for less than £250.

04 DARKROOM
- 52 LAMB'S CONDUIT STREET WC1N 3LL
- 020 7831 7244
- DARKROOMLONDON.COM
- MON-FRI 11-7, SAT 11-6, SUN, BANK HOLIDAYS 12-5
- HOLBORN/RUSSELL SQUARE

Art is design, design is fashion and fashion is art in this dark room that defies categorisation. Architectural jewellery defies wearable scale and feels substantial enough to display on the wall; angular pottery stands alone as artwork deserving of a plinth; and simple circular side tables are applied with geometric, Bauhaus-inspired embellishment that you'd never want to cover with a magazine.

In a village of independent shops on charming Lamb's Conduit Street, Darkroom stands out for its futuristic, directional feel. Laid out by the charming founders Rhonda Drakeford and Lulu Roper-Caldbeck in zones classified by primary colours, it takes you through an experience free of gender stereotypes and the traditional shopping 'departments'. A cobalt blue region displays an arrangement of tote bags, sunglasses, enamelled vases, a bowtie and arithmetical wood prints by Despina Curtis. Next it's vermilion, with Les Guimards vases, leather pouches, cushions, belts, tribal bangles – and a flame-haired shop assistant out of a Rossetti painting.

There are masterfully woven textiles sourced from Africa and hand-knitted poufs, yet their softness doesn't seem to detract from the bold, hard-edged feel of the place. They simply draw you in deeper.

05 DO

📍 34 SHORTS GARDENS WC2H 9PX

📞 020 7836 4039

↖ DO-SHOP.COM

🕐 MON 11-6:30, TUE-SAT 10-6:30, THU 10-8, SUN 12-6

⊖ COVENT GARDEN

Space doesn't come cheap in the heart of Covent Garden, which is why Do makes do with a glorified closet. Let's hope it perseveres. The people of Covent Garden deserve a place where the sole salesperson, barely able to squeeze past you to the stairs, does so in haste to find you that shelf in a different colour, and seems to know the name and provenance of a dozen new items.

Accessories come before furniture at Do, but they're the kinds of accessories that will make your life just as comfortably pleasurable as a sofa, like eccentric kitchen gadgets that work better than the stuff from your wedding list and storage solutions you didn't think you needed. Reining it in from Novelty-ville are works of artistry like the porcelain milk crate by industrial designer Alessandro Zambelli. And the brilliant French Picardie-style carafe set by Kaptein Roodnat makes an excellent gift… to yourself.

It's Europe's largest independent bookshop, but you wouldn't know it by this sombre little space in the shadow of Blackwell's and the newly expanded Foyles. Germany's Walther Koenig Books Ltd launched this presence on Bookshop Row after enjoying huge success at the Serpentine Gallery (see p.021) and, by the looks of it, book lovers have followed the scent. Koenig doesn't see huge crowds, but it doesn't have downtime either; even mid-morning is a popular hour for flicking through a hefty tome.

What's the appeal? The curating. With each opus turned out to show the cover rather than the spine, Koenig is like a museum where the artwork is the printed page. The main floor, dedicated to art volumes, is like a cross-section of London's finest galleries. Head down the narrow staircase, each stair piled with the highbrow equivalent of a remainder bin, and you'll pass a vitrine displaying rare copies. Then, at the bottom, a bounty of design, architecture and fashion titles, the likes of which you won't have spotted anywhere else.

06 KOENIG BOOKS
- 80 CHARING CROSS ROAD WC2H 0BB
- 020 7240 8190
- KOENIGBOOKS.CO.UK
- MON-FRI 11-8, SAT 10-8
- LEICESTER SQUARE

07 MAGMA
- 8 EARLHAM ST WC2H 9RY, 16 EARLHAM ST WC2H 9LN
- 020 7240 8498, 020 7240 7571
- MAGMABOOKS.COM
- MON-SAT 11-7, SUN 12-6
- LEICESTER SQUARE

It's near impossible for shops to expand in Covent Garden, so Magma Seven Dials took up digs a block down Earlham Street to house its toy and stationery selection. It's a decent formula: let the graphic design junkies flip through their design tomes and periodicals in peace at No.8, and give the frenetic shoppers more space to interact with the unusual gifts at the product shop at No.16. As a result, each shop has its own vibe and, given room to breathe, manages a quality that is scarce in the gift shops this side of Shaftesbury Avenue.

08 MOLTENI&C DADA

199 SHAFTESBURY AVENUE WC2H 8JR

020 7631 2345

MOLTENIDADA.CO.UK

MON–FRI 10-6, THU 10-8, SAT 10-5

TOTTENHAM COURT ROAD

A film director partial to fabulous urban design – Woody Allen, perhaps – would be inspired to great things by Molteni's Covent Garden flagship. If it were relocated 30 floors up, it would make the perfect penthouse set for a couple in flux who nonetheless appreciate skilful contemporary design. Molteni took over the 400-square-metre space six years ago from Christopher Wray and replaced the obstacle course of pendant lights with the expansive wall systems and sectional sofas the brand is known for.

A Molteni piece is an investment in time, space and money, as the staff here are aware, and they pay you the proper attention as you question the configurations of a mile-long floating desk by Rodolfo Dordoni or the attachments to a citrus-yellow Patricia Urquiola chaise longue. This is furniture that exudes an image that's tickety-boo, while behind are some complex workings. Allen might never stack his books with their bindings to the wall, as Molteni seems to prefer, but he would surely approve of the clever kitchens at Dada, the Italian sister brand that shares this sterling space. Perfect for eat-in intellectual gatherings.

09 MUJI
37-38 LONG ACRE WC2E 9JT
020 7379 0820
MUJI.CO.UK
MON-SAT 10-8, SUN 12-6
COVENT GARDEN

Look no further than Muji for evidence of the power of no-label. The Japanese homewares purveyor derives its name from *mujirushi ryohin*, meaning 'no-brand quality goods', and it hasn't strayed from its message since its inception in 1980. The Muji name has come to symbolise fuss-free merchandise in clean, efficient materials: stainless steel for kitchenware, porcelain for bathware, plastic for officeware and storage, and wood for furnishings. It hits the mark every time, and is thus loved by every class of consumer.

There are currently eight Muji locations throughout London – and a lot more worldwide – disproving the old adage that you've gotta have a gimmick. Here, it's the opposite. It's the old grey pullover for your décor. In fact, its grey wool convertible sofa is one of its most compelling products. And not even its Japanese product tags are putting people off. These are thoughtfully explained by the largely Japanese workforce stationed throughout the well-organised stores. You'll never regret your visit and nearly always emerge with a problem solved.

10 SOMERSET HOUSE

STRAND WC2R 1LA

020 7845 4600

SOMERSETHOUSE.ORG.UK

DAILY 10-6

COVENT GARDEN/CHARING CROSS

In lesser cities a 16th-century mansion like Somerset House would be a drain on taxpayers, an untenable relic stuffed with minor antiquities. London, however, has learned to get the most out of its monuments. The one-time venue for the Hermitage Rooms, the estate is now a hub for contemporary creatives, housing a slew of cultural organisations like the British Fashion Council, which lobbied successfully to hold the majority of runway shows here during London Fashion Week, and the Sorrell Foundation, which aims to inspire kids through good design.

Today, Somerset House operates round the clock. Office workers pick up their morning lattes at a branch of Fernandez & Wells, then come back for lunch at Tom's Kitchen. The Impressionist-rich Courtauld Gallery and contemporary East Wing galleries showcase top art exhibits throughout the week. And the multi-acre courtyard, dotted with vigorous fountains in summer, hosts the most romantic ice-skating venue in the land come Christmas. Walk the corridors of the West Wing and descend to the Embankment Galleries for a changing programme of contemporary exhibitions. Or lose an hour in the Rizzoli bookshop, a treat in the literary wasteland of the Strand.

And still people return at night for outdoor cinema, live-music events or simply to behold the view of the Thames from the Terrace, one of London's most sublime spots.

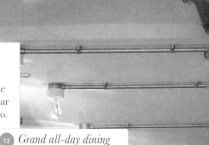

11 *A room be to seen in*

New York's most famous restaurant opened in London in 2013. High ceilings, red banquets and Parisian style in former Theatre Museum. Brasserie menu served throughout the day, but head to the bar for their burger and fries. Top bakery next door, too.

BALTHAZAR LONDON 4-6 RUSSELL STREET WC2B 5HZ
020 3301 1155 | BALTHAZARLONDON.COM

● ● ●   ●

12 *Grand all-day dining*

Dark green banquettes, black and white tiled floor, wood panelled walls, exceptional service at this very 'grand café'. All-day menu ranges from hotdogs and salt-beef pretzels to oysters and caviar.

THE DELAUNAY 55 ALDWYCH WC2B 4BB
020 7499 8558 | THEDELAUNAY.COM

◑ ● ●   ● ● ●

13 *Artisan gelato*

All natural Italian gelato handmade using seasonal ingredients. Original arched window into small and friendly café and ice cream parlour. These guys are seriously passionate about ice cream.

LA GELATIERA 27 NEW ROW WC2N 4LA
020 7836 9559 | LAGELATIERA.CO.UK

● ● ●

14 *French cooking*

Influenced by produce and recipes from the Loire river. Old pub converted into stunning bistro-style eatery with dining bar. Beautiful cooking and extensive wine list. Sister to wonderful Terroirs further down the road.

GREEN MAN AND FRENCH HORN [PICTURED] 54 ST MARTINS LN
WC2N 4EA | 020 7836 2645 | GREENMANFRENCHHORN.CO

● ● ●   ● ● ●

15 *Institutional appeal*

Legendary oyster bar and spanking bivalve bistro. Art Deco mini-palace. Smoky mirrors with orange sconces, monochrome photos of faded actors, Orient Express-style table lamps. Glamorous, chic and charming with exemplary service.

J. SHEEKEY 28-24 ST MARTIN'S COURT WC2N 4AL
020 7240 2565 | J-SHEEKEY.CO.UK

● ● ●   ● ● ●

16 Fusion flavours

All-day restaurant and café from Kiwi chef Peter Gordon, serving some of the best food in the area. Casual dining experience for every occasion with high-calibre flavours. A treasure in a tourist area.

KOPAPA 32-34 MONMOUTH STREET WC2H 9HA
020 7240 6076 | KOPAPA.CO.UK

17 Selection of coffees

Small, personal coffee house roasting and retailing coffee since 1978. Fight your way in for a table in the tiny seating area, or grab & go. Range of pastries and cakes to complement the finest coffee.

MONMOUTH COFFEE COMPANY 27 MONMOUTH ST WC2H 9EU
020 7379 3516 | MONMOUTHCOFFEE.CO.UK

18 Old Fashioned

Said to be the oldest restaurant in London, this place is a classic. But it's the dark wood bar upstairs that is the real find. Expert bartenders make the perfect martini or Old Fashioned with style and flare.

RULES 34 MAIDEN LANE WC2E 7LB
020 7836 5314 | RULES.CO.UK

19 Best burger

Famous burger shack from NYC finally arrives in London. All-natural burgers, flat-top dogs, frozen custard, beer, wine and more. Join the C-line to find out what all the fuss is about.

SHAKE SHACK 24 MARKET BUILDING, THE PIAZZA WC2E 8RD
SHAKESHACK.COM

Place to sleep? 20

COVENT GARDEN HOTEL FIRMDALEHOTELS.COM

STORYTELLING *continued from p.091*

I'm interested in personality – I could be with a customer for an hour, chatting and explaining things.

NEIL SAUNDERS

I think that most retailers recognise that less is more now, and it isn't just about providing loads and loads of stuff, it's about providing the right stuff for the people. For smaller niche players, that has always been easier because you have a personality there, whereas if you are a big player you don't always have that flexibility and it presents a massive step change in the way you do business.

MAX FRASER

Does anybody want to comment on the reach and power of social media and if and how that has benefited your sales and revenues?

RHONDA DRAKEFORD

We have spent a lot of time on that recently and I think that we're still trying to work out whether it's worth the time investment. I think that it's more about brand building than sales.

MIA THITTICHAI

I do think it's quite useful in the quieter moments to shout out some of your own news, but also to see what people are talking about at particular times. It does enable you to stay quite close to the beat and I think there are more ways that it can work for us.

MAX FRASER

It's important to establish your own conversational tone so that people don't feel like you're flogging them something but instead you're educating them or driving them to some interesting information.

NEIL SAUNDERS

The double edge sword is that it's very public as well, so

SOCIAL MEDIA

…if you get something wrong (be it a product or customer service), it's very easy for somebody to take a picture of it or tweet it and that could potentially be damaging.

As a big retailer you have to be very controlling and you have to be aware of how you will deal with it. If you don't deal with it in an appropriate way, a very little problem that once could have been dealt with in store, has suddenly become a massive problem that everyone can see and it's detrimental to your brand.

STAFF

MAX FRASER

How difficult is it to recruit and retain good, knowledgeable staff?

MAGNUS ENGLUND

It is very difficult because retail has a low status. We try to train staff and give them incentives to keep them within the company, but it is not that easy. Also, people have relatively low expectations of what they're going to get from the business.

RHONDA DRAKEFORD

I suppose you look for people who have the interest and knowledge on a personal level so that they want to learn about what they are selling.

SHERIDAN COAKLEY

I think that most of the staff that we've had have all had some kind of design background. For a lot of furniture designers it's just so hard to earn a living, so it's one way to get connected with the business.

MAX FRASER

Do any of you have tactics for sustaining morale around your staff and rewarding success?

RHONDA DRAKEFORD

We tend to bond over alcohol and nights out!

NEIL SAUNDERS

I don't think that it is any coincidence that one of the most successful retailers with the longest average service is John Lewis, because the way that they incentivise staff is by letting them own a share. The one thing they may possibly lack is the passion from their people. And that is what you do get from the independent stores, especially if it's an owner-run business.

SHERIDAN COAKLEY

Then on the contract side of the business, staff are kept incentivised by commission. That marks a massive difference between the retail and the contract markets, as it comes down to how much people earn.

Continued p.124

BAGNODESIGN
LONDON

Designers And Manufacturers of Unique Bathroom Solutions
31 Pear Tree Street, Clerkenwell, London, EC1V 3AG, United Kingdom
TEL: +44 (0)20 7553 6999   e: info@bagnodesign.co.uk   www.bagnodesign.co.uk

Clerkenwell
& Finsbury

EC1
E.C.2

↑ Islington | p.128

→ Shoreditch & Brick Lane | p.144

- Design galleries & institutions
- Design shops & C2oth vintage
- Design bookshops

- Eat & drink (pp.122-123)

01 ARPER
02 BARBICAN ART GALLERY
03 FØREST LONDON
04 GN FURNITURE
05 .IT ALL ABOUT DESIGN
06 KNOLL
07 MAGMA
08 MODUS
09 MOROSO/FLOS
10 POLTRONA FRAU GROUP

11 PRESENT & CORRECT
12 TIMOROUS BEASTIES
13 TWENTYTWENTYONE
14 VIADUCT
15 VITRA
16 ZAHA HADID DESIGN GALLERY

Street*wise*

When did you move to this street?
We moved here in April 1997.

What originally attracted you to it?
We met over a charcoal grill in The Eagle pub on Farringdon Road, where we both worked 18 years ago. We knew the area, and we knew there were plenty of foodies in the area. This was a part of town we could afford, as Exmouth Market was very run down and the landlord who owns most of the street was offering very attractive rents to encourage businesses.

How has this thoroughfare changed since you've been here?
We were told that we were mad to open a restaurant on Exmouth Market, but over the last 16 years we have seen the market prosper and flourish hugely. The once disused and empty shops have been replaced by independent and varied businesses, many from Soho and the West End.

What does the street offer the community that is unique?
A microcosm of the best of London; multi-ethnic, varied and diverse with a great energy. It offers everything from the best coffee in London from Brill or Caravan, to a tattoo from The Family Business. There is beautiful jewellery from EC One, as well as great independent shops, such as handbag designers Bagman & Robin and lifestyle shop Family Tree. You can finish a great day shopping by playing a game of table football while having a beer at Café Kick.

Tell us about some of your neighbouring hotspots.
The Quality Chop House around the corner on Farringdon Road is great for a glass of wine and a bite; it's been there since 1869. I'm quite partial to a Vietnamese pork baguette from Bun Cha. And Bookends is one of the best children's bookshops in London.

What has recently changed on neighbouring roads that has alarmed you?
We were sad when Clarks, the traditional pie and eel shop, closed after many many years due to the rent increase. On the last day there was a queue that snaked right down to the end of the street!

If you could change one thing on the street, what would it be?
We were very excited by a proposal from local architects Tonkin Liu, who put forward a proposal in 2011 to resurface Exmouth Market with a charming design that encourages pedestrian and outside living, and creates gateways at two ends of the market with trees and lighting. Fingers crossed that, as and when funding becomes available, phases of the project may progress.

Sam & Sam Clarke
Moro

34-36 EXMOUTH MARKET EC1R 4QE
020 7833 8787 MORO.CO.UK

EXMOUTH MARKET

01 ARPER
📍 11 CLERKENWELL ROAD EC1M 5PA
📞 020 7253 0009
↖ ARPER.COM
🕐 MON-FRI 9:30-6
⊖ FARRINGDON

Arper seems to be a follower of the Uniqlo school of merchandising, in which a single item is displayed in a spectrum of colours to increase its appeal. The furniture here has that Italian structural integrity; since its young days in the 1990s, the company has had a reputation for hiring brilliant design thinkers like Rodolfo Dordoni, who spent years researching the construction of a single chair. It's up to you whether the look trumps the wares at Vitra across the road or other competitors beyond.

The 2012 arrival of Arper is a welcome addition amid the raft of other slick furniture showrooms that populate this area. Principally aimed at the trade, members of the public are nevertheless free to explore. The open-plan space was designed by 6A Architects as a show-meeting-event-exhibition space in an up-to-the-moment mix of bleached wood, cast aluminium and industrial concrete. It reflects the precision with which Arper designs its furniture lines, the most popular of which are the new *Pix* ottomans by Iwasaki, and Lievore Altherr Molina's *Duna*, *Leaf* and *Catifa* chairs, which made Arper famous.

02 BARBICAN ART GALLERY

SILK STREET EC2Y 8DS

020 7638 4141

BARBICAN.ORG.UK/ARTGALLERY

MON–TUE, FRI–SUN 11–8, WED 11–6, THU 11–10

BARBICAN/MOORGATE

Like a fortress within the city, the towering Barbican complex is disconcertingly awkward to access, surrounded as it is by tunnels, detours, bridges and a prohibitive one-way system. Once you do get in, though, it's like a field day in concrete. Architects Chamberlin, Powell & Bon built the complex in the 1960s and '70s as a social utopia, a place where families could live safely within walking distance of work and school, and interact with neighbours in umpteen communal spaces. There are terraces and gardens at every level, duck ponds and fountains, restaurants and cafés, and multiple foyers furnished for gatherings, large or intimate.

Love it or hate it, as Londoners are wont to do, the Barbican is a masterpiece of the Brutalist style, with monolithic residential towers and low-rises where teams of builders actually chipped away at the cast concrete to give it an irregular modernist texture. In 2001, English Heritage gave it a Grade-II listing, right down to the teak windowpanes and kitchen sinks customised by yacht-builders. And since then, its public art facility, the Barbican Centre, has blossomed. The cosy cinemas host film festivals and events; the performance halls attract massive talent; the free-of-charge Curve gallery is queued up even on Monday mornings; and the second-floor Barbican Art Gallery does battle with the V&A and National Portrait Gallery for top architecture, design, art and photography exhibitions.

Forest launched in 2012 as a home for northern European midcentury antiques styled with unparalleled warmth and grace by Dutch fashion merchandising grad Eva Coppens. Her devotion to Dutch and Scandi greats like Friso Kramer, Pastoe and Kai Kristiansen goes back to her life in Holland. Now London-based, she is familiar with the commute by van and restores her haul expertly, often reupholstering with new graphic fabrics by local Londoner Tamasyn Gambell.

Competition for contemporary is fierce around here, so it's no wonder Coppens doesn't tolerate scuffs or old rings in the wood. Her stock is impeccable and original, dainty enough for petite City flats and often blessed with concealed doors and shelves. Plus the prices are a reprieve from those of her Clerkenwell neighbours; you could do quite well with £500, for instance, picking up a coffee table, dresser or chair with change leftover for a new cushion designed by Coppens in collaboration with Holly May.

03 FØREST LONDON

- 115 CLERKENWELL ROAD EC1R 5BY
- 07535 637 731
- WWW.FORESTLONDON.COM
- MON-FRI 11-7, SAT 12-5
- FARRINGDON

04 GN FURNITURE

- 31 EXMOUTH MARKET EC1R 4QL
- 020 7833 0370
- GNFURNITURE.CO.UK
- MON-SAT 12-6, SUN 12-5
- FARRINGDON/ANGEL

When GN opened a few years back in this lively island of gentrification in Farringdon, I thought: What took you so long? A midcentury lifestyle boutique just seems to belong on this continental strip of tapas, foosball and vinyl sellers. Alas the answer is in the real estate – the terraced houses are simply too narrow for much stock. Shoppers carrying as little as a shoulder bag will get stuck, quite literally, into the depths of GN.

That's not to say there aren't some treats in here. There's Anglepoise lighting on tap, unusual framed artworks and pretty retro-look ceramics by Vicky Thornton. The teak Danish-modern furniture is in great condition too, alongside British collectibles from Ercol, Hille and Isokon. If you're hunting for something particular, feel free to enquire and they will help source it.

05 .IT ALL ABOUT DESIGN

📍 20-22 ROSEBERY AVENUE EC1R 4SX

📞 020 3119 1111

🔗 PUNTOIT.CO.UK

🕐 MON-FRI 9:30-6:30

🚇 FARRINGDON/CHANCERY LANE

If Moroso/Flos across the street is the Milanese eccentric, IT is its more urbane older sibling, offering a little more sheen, a little more decadence and a wine bar to set the mood. The space is cavernous and convivial, and young Europeans congregate on the deep modular sofas – to the point that you're not sure if they're shopping or working.

.IT calls itself a multi-brand concept store, but I fail to see where the 'concept' comes in. There are a few oddball pieces and a handful of brands you won't find elsewhere, but the sterile metal fixtures read a bit corporate. The company deals largely with the trade, and it seems to show.

06 KNOLL

📍 91 GOSWELL ROAD EC1V 7EX

📞 020 7236 6655

🔗 KNOLL-INT.COM

🕐 MON-FRI 9-5:30

🚇 BARBICAN

It's easy to forget amid the new-furniture scent at Knoll's pristine London HQ that there are 75 years of history under this roof, the product of Hans Knoll's business savvy, his wife Florence's ties to Mies van der Rohe and the enduring designs of modernists like Jens Risom and Eero Saarinen. The founders believed that modern architects would need modern furniture to make their buildings liveable so they nurtured the most talented designers of their time to fulfil this.

The company is blessed with a portfolio of 20th century classics that have graced the finest interiors for multiple decades, and continue to do so. There are few spaces that wouldn't be bettered with the addition of a Mies van der Rohe *Barcelona* chair. The entire collection – if you can afford it – has a flawless elegance that's like fine art for devotees of modernist design.

This location is like a gallery in which the craft is given room to breath, space for you to admire it from all angles. And as a reminder of its rich heritage, it also hosts the occasional exhibition or provocative debate to support the exchange of ideas.

07 MAGMA

- 117-119 CLERKENWELL ROAD EC1R 5BY
- 020 7242 9503
- MAGMABOOKS.COM
- MON-SAT 10-7
- FARRINGDON

It's been a pleasure to watch Magma, purveyors of arty books, magazines and miscellany, expand from its first location in Covent Garden (see p.100) to this Clerkenwell branch. It's also a pleasure to report that the place hasn't grown up too much. It still does guilty-pleasure typography tomes and pictogram T-shirts, and a kids' section that blends in with the adults' because the toys appeal to everyone. Since the city has fallen for graphic design, Magma seems much less niche and more accessible to anyone in search of a unique gift. And if you're looking for the graphic novel that geeky guy from your printmaking class recently put out on an obscure imprint, they'll likely have that, too. Thank you to Magma for helping to keep high quality print publications relevant and alive.

08 MODUS

- 28-29 GREAT SUTTON STREET EC1V 0DS
- 020 7490 1358
- MODUSFURNITURE.CO.UK
- MON-FRI 10-6
- FARRINGDON/BARBICAN

If there was ever any question whether Britain could compete with the other big-name European manufacturers populating the Clerkenwell Design District, the Modus showroom gives an emphatic 'yes'. The home-grown company, founded in 2000, has launched some of the most memorable designer collaborations in recent years, not least due to its dedication to tapping local talent, as well as a growing number of international names.

The tiny Clerkenwell floor has a stripped-back chic courtesy of Modus creative director Michael Sodeau, all the better for displaying the latest merchandise, like Magnus Long's clever *Bend* bench. Recently I also had a go on Stephen Burks's super-smart *Pleats* sofa, encouraged to stay as long as I wished by an assistant who wasn't expecting my subsequent onslaught of questions.

If the folks at Moroso don't mind me saying, the London location is a barrel of fun for children. It's doubtful the inexhaustible Spanish designer Patricia Urquiola had this in mind when she dreamed up this Barbarella-mod space – a foil for the Victorian arches of Rosebery Avenue. Still, she's injected it with an otherworldly wonder.

Furniture producer Moroso has a reputation for getting designers to let their eccentricities hang out. Perhaps a recession-busting endeavour, it joined forces with fellow Italian lighting brand Flos in this expansive Clerkenwell showroom space. The partnership is still standing, though given the lack of attention I got on a recent walk-in, it would appear the bulk of its business still comes from high-volume contract work.

Unsurprisingly, Urquiola's designs for Flos and Moroso get pride of place here, colourful and eye-catching as they are; when she launched her woven-plastic *Tatou* lamps for Flos in 2012, they rained down on the flagship like hailstones. Whatever is on display when you visit, be assured that you're looking at high-quality future collectibles designed by today's leading talents.

09 MOROSO/FLOS
7-15 ROSEBERY AVENUE EC1R 4SP
020 3328 3560
MOROSO.IT, FLOS.COM
MON-FRI 9-5
FARRINGDON/CHANCERY LANE

Poltrona Frau is at the top of its game, and that's truly saying something after 100 years in the exceedingly competitive business of modern Italian furniture. In the days since commissioning groundbreaking designs from Jean Nouvel, Richard Meier and Pierluigi Cerri, one of Milan's most prolific designers, the company has been on a winning streak. The millennium began with the acquisition of Gebrüder Thonet, followed by fellow Italian manufacturers Cappellini and Cassina. And in the past decade it has opened flagships across Europe.

This is one of a dozen temples to Italian interiors in Clerkenwell, but Poltrona Frau doesn't get lost in this elegant Victorian warehouse on St John Street. It has the lure of a boutique, with intimate room sets (Cappellini and Cassina dominate) demonstrating the visual heft of its stock. The only hint of its multinational status is the glamorous meeting room downstairs – often populated by polished Europeans discussing their next prestige collaboration.

10 POLTRONA FRAU GROUP
150 ST JOHN STREET EC1V 4UD
020 7014 5980
POLTRONAFRAUGROUP.COM
MON-FRI 8:30-5:30
FARRINGDON/BARBICAN

11 PRESENT & CORRECT
23 ARLINGTON WAY EC1R 1UY
020 7278 2460
PRESENTANDCORRECT.COM
TUE–FRI 12–6:30
ANGEL

The more advanced our touch-type technology becomes, the more some of us (with time on our hands and money in our pockets) go the other way. Rymans could disappear and we wouldn't bat an eye, but places like the new Present & Correct are fuel for our backlash against communicating through the ether.

Ironically, this stationer, founded by Neal Whittington, began online in 2008 before going old school this year with a cute space in a sweet Georgian terrace in the villagey shopping strip behind Sadler's Wells. It turns out there was quite a demand for office supplies – workable staplers, heavy tape dispensers, quality pencils – that are disappearing from the wider world but still rather handy. Present & Correct avoids the sparkly twee-ness of chains like Paperchase, opting for a look that nods to the past while agreeing with our contemporary expectations of design.

There are desktop supplies in delicious colours, and accordion files that win awards at design shows. You can find old toys like the reissued Speak & Spell of my youth, a vintage Olivetti Valentine typewriter and tin geometry sets, and well-considered stationery like letterpress labels and splendid notebooks to keep in stacks for inspiration. Rarely is an item more than £20 – except the Olivetti, of course. But that folds into a jaunty red case with a handle, so £295 is really a bargain for such a design classic.

12 TIMOROUS BEASTIES

- 46 AMWELL STREET EC1R 1XS
- 020 7833 5010
- TIMOROUSBEASTIES.COM
- MON–SAT 10–6
- ANGEL

The beasties running Timorous's only English flagship (the other is in Glasgow) have all the time in the world for you – not because they're not busy, but because they're passionate. They'll point out the weft of a weave, the hand-painted overlay of a digital print, the unreplicated design on a wallpaper roll, the scene you might have missed on their outrageous London toile.

The Scottish duo Alistair McAuley and Paul Simmons have cornered the market in natural scenes (on natural fibres) with a decidedly contemporary – even macabre – edge. They were doing Rorschach blotch prints eons before McQueen and other fashion designers caught on to their appeal. A salesman gives an affected sniff when I deign to bring up the fashion legacy.

Lately the outfit has launched a line of truly original exterior design products concrete tiles printed with garden scenes by London moulders Graphic Relief.

13 TWENTYTWENTYONE SHOWROOM

- 18C RIVER STREET EC1R 1XN
- 020 7837 1900
- TWENTYTWENTYONE.COM
- MON–SAT 9:30–5:30
- ANGEL

Amwell Village is one of the more pleasant places to mooch around on a bright afternoon, not least because of the quaint 19th-century spaces transformed into showrooms that work for the 21st. The area is resoundingly local, and you'll certainly feel like you have some local nous turning the corner into this nugget of a shop.

Twentytwentyone also has a shopfront on the high-footfall boulevard of Upper Street (p.137), but here you get more freedom and more space to test out the big-impact lighting and the range of classic chairs from leading European brands – plus the vast modern sofas and rugs you won't find at the smaller location.

If you're moved by a Knoll *Credenza* or a *Mega* armchair by Chris Martin, you won't have to fumble around for your hazards or wangle a parking pass – there's space galore here to pull up and fill the boot.

14 VIADUCT

1-10 SUMMERS STREET EC1R 5BD

020 7278 8456

VIADUCT.CO.UK

MON-FRI 9:30-6, SAT 10:30-4

FARRINGDON

A timeless, clean-lined aesthetic transcends all of the products on display in this double-height, converted 1930s print house.

The contract market makes up the majority of Viaduct's business so staff will often be attending to the demands of an interior designer or architect. But this shouldn't put off members of the public hunting for a special addition for their home. Viaduct employees are incredibly knowledgeable about the vast range of items they sell. Tell them the sort of item that you're looking for and they will propose many potential options. Alternatively, enjoy a cheerful spin around the space, taking in E15's flawless *Enoki* marble-topped tables or perfectly formed wooden *Hiroshima* armchairs by Naoto Fukasawa.

Most of the European contemporaries in the neighbourhood are diversifying from bare-bones austerity, but Viaduct does it with aplomb, partly due to its penchant for heavy-metal sophistication: Tom Dixon's copper and pressed-glass pendants, and Philipp Mainzer's brass and copper *Habibi* tray tables, to name a few. Viaduct thankfully transcends the trends, selling a well-considered selection of what owner James Mair and his team have sourced internationally.

15 VITRA

30 CLERKENWELL ROAD EC1M 5PQ

020 7608 6200

VITRA.COM

MON-THU 9-5:30, FRI 9-5

FARRINGDON

Sitting in an office cubicle is hardly the stuff of fantasy – unless, that is, Vitra has had a hand in designing it. The Swiss-owned company, founded in the mid-20th century to license designs by Charles and Ray Eames and George Nelson for the European market, made its name transforming office landscapes, and more recently hired Ronan and Erwan Bouroullec to design *The Workbay Office* that's entirely customisable by the employee. Even its stand-alone home-office desks are a revelation: *Tyde*, designed in 2012 by the Bouroullec brothers, also works as a drafting table, stand-up desk or boardroom table.

The company has been in the domestic trade for over a decade now, and the Clerkenwell showroom has softened its edges with top lighting from Noguchi and Frank Gehry, whose *Cloud* lamps set the tone on the ground floor. It has made a star of Hella Jongerius and her *Polder* sofa, and it introduced the late Maarten Van Severen's *Kast* storage system in 2005.

You can't buy direct from this showroom, but the public are welcome to browse the collections and staff will inform you of your nearest dealer should you wish to place an order. And do keep an eye out for the infamous mid-winter one-day-only sale, when people are known to camp overnight to pick up some incredible bargains.

16 ZAHA HADID DESIGN GALLERY

101 GOSWELL ROAD EC1V 7EZ

020 7253 5147

ZAHA-HADID-DESIGN.COM

TUES-SAT 12-6

BARBICAN

For decades, Zaha Hadid was the UK's most prominent architect without a completed building in her home country. As the wider world began to implement her fluid, multi-faceted designs – and after she won the 2004 Pritzker Prize – it became clear Hadid could be great beyond the computer screen. Less than 10 years on, her architecture has begun to colonise the country: the Maggie's Centre in Fife, the Roca London Gallery (p.199), the breathtaking Olympic Aquatics Centre.

Hadid's household designs, commissioned by manufacturers like Alessi (p.068) and Established & Sons (p.132) or created for galleries like David Gill (p.070), enjoyed a lower profile until the recent launch of her Clerkenwell gallery. Having them all in one place, we are finally able to gain some insight into her spatial experimentation.

The space has been left raw, save for a staircase descending like a series of vertebrae. Upstairs are her vast sweeps of furniture, so dizzying to wander around, you rue the no-touch policy as you seek somewhere to steady yourself. Prices run to the tens of thousands, and you might see why, considering the deft ergonomics and hidden storage. Downstairs is an array of swooping tabletop designs and jewellery, the function of which you'll have to enlist an assistant to explain. Most edifying is a stepped cardboard sculpture that comes as close to a model of her mindset as you'll get.

17 *Brunch & coffee*

Popular restaurant, bar and roaster run by a friendly
New Zealand team. Superb coffee, hearty brunches,
imaginative, Kiwi-inspired tapas dishes. Now has a
new outpost in regenerated King's Cross.

CARAVAN 11–13 EXMOUTH MARKET EC1R 4QD
020 7833 8115 | CARAVANONEXMOUTH.CO.UK

18 *Hearty gastro dishes*

The first gastropub is over 20 years old now and still
going strong. Serves consistently brilliant, original
dishes in generous portions. Great energy, no
reservations so be prepared to fight for a table! Open
kitchen with North African influences, great value.

THE EAGLE 159 FARRINGDON ROAD EC1R 3AL
020 7837 1353

19 *Original flavours*

Exciting fusion menu with a touch of Antipodean
exotica, chef/owner Anna Hansen is a half Danish,
half Canadian Kiwi. Stunning townhouse with
café, dining rooms and outside seating in the square.
Open all day.

THE MODERN PANTRY 47-48 ST JOHN'S SQUARE EC1V 4JJ
020 7553 9210 | THEMODERNPANTRY.CO.UK

20 *Spanish bites*

Little sister to brilliant Moro next door. Jostle
for space at the bright-orange Formica bar
overlooking the open kitchen. Delicious small plates
complemented by choice sherries.

MORITO 32 EXMOUTH MARKET EC1R 4QE
020 7278 7007 | MORITO.CO.UK

21 *Modern day dining*

Bangkok café 'serving an eclectic menu of dishes
from the East to West'. Alan Yau's contemporary
eatery open for breakfast, lunch, dinner and all day
for coffee and desserts. Set menus, rice and noodle
dishes, grills and salads, even a burger or two.

NAAMYAA CAFÉ 407 ST JOHN STREET EC1V 4AB
020 3122 0988 | NAAMYAA.COM

22 A bit of Venetian style

Another Russell Norman success story. Negroni's
and Aperol Spritz at the bar, small well-priced
Italian dishes, *fritto misto* and *arancini* are a must.
Exposed brickwork, wooden tables with a Venice
via New York vibe.

POLPO SMITHFIELD 3 COWCROSS STREET EC1M 6DR
020 7250 0034 | POLPO.CO.UK

23 Nose to tail

Wood floors, whitewash walls and vaulted ceilings
in this old smokehouse building with restaurant, bar
and private room. World famous, gutsy, nose-to-tail
eating from Fergus Henderson, meat from the local
market and daily-changing menu.

ST JOHN 26 ST JOHN STREET EC1M 4AY
020 3301 8069 | STJOHNRESTAURANT.COM

24 Tea & cake

Popular with the local fashion and publishing
crowd, a good space to work with iPads positioned
on workbenches. Sofas and armchairs on the lower
floor. Artisan teas and good coffee, cakes and
sandwiches are on offer.

TIMBERYARD 61-67 OLD STREET EC1V 9HW
TIMBERYARDLONDON.COM

25 The perfect coffee

Bustling café and roaster with good menus, brunch
dishes are particularly appetising. Square central
coffee 'bar', exposed brick walls, roaster in view and
wall of plants give the space an indoor-outdoor feel.

WORKSHOP COFFEE CO 27 CLERKENWELL ROAD EC1M 5RN
020 7253 5754 | WORKSHOPCOFFEE.COM

26 Eccentric Britishness

Cosy, eccentric, cocktail lounge on the ground floor
of this townhouse hotel serves excellent cocktails by
Tony Conigliaro, small plates from Bruno Loubet
across the road. Happily spend all night here.

THE ZETTER TOWNHOUSE 49-50 ST JOHN'S SQUARE EC1V 4JJ
COCKTAIL LOUNGE 020 7324 4545
THEZETTERTOWNHOUSE.COM

Place to sleep? 26

THE ZETTER TOWNHOUSE THEZETTERTOWNHOUSE.COM

Continued from p.107

MAX FRASER

As customers become more knowledgeable, do you have to go to greater lengths to source new products?

JAMES MAIR

Yes, definitely, I think in terms of travelling the world searching for new products, and because we can all travel easily. Wherever we go, we each have our own individual tastes to guide us.

MAGNUS ENGLUND

I think every retailer's dream is to find a new great product that nobody else has, and that earns you a good margin and that nobody else sells.

LINA KANAFANI

… and the internet has never heard of it.

SHERIDAN COAKLEY

I enjoy finding new stuff as I think it is part of the fun, and we are all hoping that these products will have longevity. You do need that novelty aspect and you need to find something that is fresh and different.

MAX FRASER

Have you noticed any change to your suppliers' terms recently?

LINA KANAFANI

Prices have gone up.

MAGNUS ENGLUND

They are keener to get paid on time.

SHERIDAN COAKLEY

Smaller companies want you to pay them up front and that has become much more normal within Europe – it definitely has shifted.

MAX FRASER

And do any of you ask for consignment from your suppliers?

RHONDA DRAKEFORD

We do – all of our jewellery is sale-or-return (SOR). For some reason, jewellery works in that way and you don't feel guilty asking for it.

LINA KANAFANI

Yes, I will always ask for consignment.

MAX FRASER

The designers and brands I talk to are increasingly frustrated by this consignment demand because they feel that all of the financial risk rests on their shoulders with no guarantee of a return.

SOURCING PRODUCTS

JAMES MAIR

I think that's a shame because often you're very enthusiastic about a certain designer and want to support them. In Lina's case, their work could be very experimental so she doesn't want to take any risk unnecessarily, but equally, she wants to add it to the marketplace. So it's swings and roundabouts for every individual.

JUSTIN PRATT

But then the retailer is providing show space, which is their offering. It should all be mutually beneficial.

PROVENANCE

MAX FRASER

Let's talk about the provenance of a product – is the 'Made in Britain/Italy/Sweden' etc important today?

MAGNUS ENGLUND

Increasingly so, more and more customers ask if it is made in China or not.

LINA KANAFANI

Not really because they either like a design or not. They do not think about where it has come from.

SHERIDAN COAKLEY

More people factor in if it's made in the UK.

MAX FRASER

Sheridan, you play to those strengths in your communications.

SHERIDAN COAKLEY

Well, we try to. For example, it works well with our pottery factory where we produce in Stoke-on-Trent, but we are at a very privileged end of the market. Producing furniture in the UK is a very difficult thing to do, but I have proceeded on the basis that somebody can always make something cheaper elsewhere so we go for quality instead. There's no point trying to flog a dead horse; I think that producing certain things in the UK just doesn't work.

SIMON ALDERSON

It becomes part of your specialisation that your team can communicate about how something is manufactured and the materials

Continued p.140

Islington

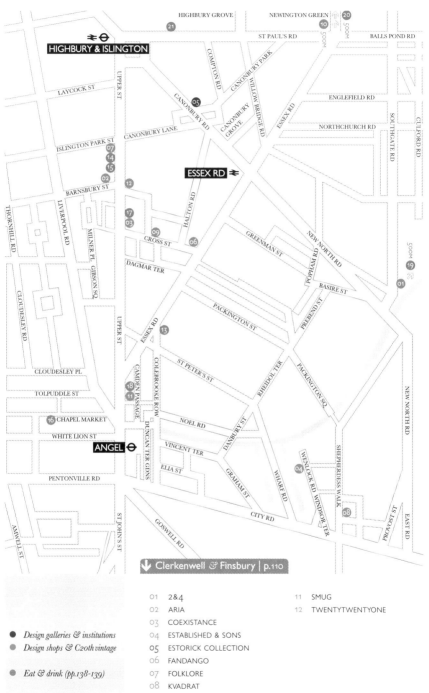

01 2&4
02 ARIA
03 COEXISTANCE
04 ESTABLISHED & SONS
05 ESTORICK COLLECTION
06 FANDANGO
07 FOLKLORE
08 KVADRAT
09 LAGO ISLINGTON
10 THE PEANUT VENDOR

11 SMUG
12 TWENTYTWENTYONE

● *Design galleries & institutions*
● *Design shops & C20th vintage*

● *Eat & drink (pp.138-139)*

Street*wise*

When did you move to this street?
I opened my design shop Smug in June 2009.

What originally attracted you to it?
I grew up spending my pocket money on little trinkets in the Camden Passage antiques market so I've always had a soft spot for it. It seemed to me in 2008 that the passage might be about to start regenerating itself but would need a little push. So I pushed. Luckily for me, others were doing the same.

How has this shopping thoroughfare and surrounding area changed since you've been here?
It's been a shame, as many have noted, to see the antiques trade diminish slightly, but I love what is still left and enjoy the new balance of little design shops, cafés and bars in the context of an antiques market in the heart of a community.

What does the street offer the community that is unique?
Well we certainly have a few eccentrics! A pedestrianised street always offers such a nice pace of life to an area and Camden Passage is no exception. Those in the know choose to mooch along the passage taking in the atmosphere and avoid the noise and chains of the main road nearby.

Tell us about some of your neighbouring hotspots.
I love Paul A Young and Fat Faced Cat. Paul's salted milk chocolate is the best around and I use my monogrammed vintage leather satchel from FFC every day. I feel as though I practically live at Ottolenghi's restaurant, which is just up the road on Upper Street. Aesop on Cross Street is a favourite, too.

What has recently changed on neighbouring roads that has alarmed you?
It's always a shame to see businesses fail or the occasional wrong sort of chain store moving in, but in general I'm very proud of what Islington has to offer its residents.

If you could change one thing on the street, what would it be?
I'd love my end of the passage to be a bit more awake. The established antiques shops do so well that they only need to open on Wednesdays and Saturdays which can sometimes make things feel a little sleepy. I wouldn't want to change the midweek chilled atmosphere for anything too dynamic though as the passage is already pretty lively on the weekends so I should be careful what I wish for. Let's just go with more outside benches for people to sit and have coffee on. Maybe Smug should get one…

Lizzie Evans
Smug

13 CAMDEN PASSAGE N1 8EA
020 7354 0253 IFEELSMUG.COM

CAMDEN PASSAGE

01 2&4

- 2-4 SOUTHGATE ROAD N1 3JW
- 020 7254 5202
- 2MDESIGN.CO.UK
- TUE-FRI 9-6.30, SAT 10-6, SUN 11-5
- HAGGERSTON

When you have a potential buyer coming round to your house, bake some bread, the saying goes. Well, 2&4 has gone one further and placed its café at the front of house, so you can't avoid the aromas of brewing soup and fresh-ground coffee. If you're ravenous, perhaps you'll stay for some. If not, at least it adds value to a snoop around the furniture showroom.

The canalside space, on the main floor of the old Thomas Briggs army tent factory, is expansive in size and scope, an airy setting for midcentury oak sideboards, retro teaware and seating from the 1970s onward. It might be written off as your average vintage repository if not for the lighting and glasswork thrown into the mix. Owners Maurice Nugent and Mia Fihnborg design ceramics, glass and furnishings on the side through their company 2M, and the vibrant, modestly priced designs – pendant lights, decorative mirrors and glass art, mostly – give the furnishings a contemporary context.

They're also helping to revive this down-at-heel junction, making it a pleasant place to linger – something that's eluded the developers of the new residential highrises up the road.

02 ARIA

BARNSBURY HALL, BARNSBURY STREET N1 1PN

020 7704 6222

ARIASHOP.CO.UK

MON-SAT 10-6:30, SUN 12-5

HIGHBURY & ISLINGTON

It's been a mainstay in the area since the first bankers arrived in their Beemers on the shores of Canonbury and Barnsbury. Back then, Aria delivered Alessi serving pieces and Kartell gnomes and were welcome migrants to this world of Georgian townhouses where the most notable retail was the antiques strip to the south. Originally sited on Upper Street, in the late Noughties Aria moved to Barnsbury Hall up the road. Beautifully restored, respecting the vaulted gothic ceilings and Georgian brick while modernising with light wells, the multi-storey space has likewise modernised its stock, turning its attentions to lifestyle brands by introducing more aspirational European furnishings (though Kartell is still a stock favourite), pricey rugs, Paul Smith accessories and a library of design tomes.

If you can afford it and count yourself among the growing group of contemporary-design aficionados in London, you can have fun here. The building itself is a joy, with different nooks and levels to explore. 2014 marks a new chapter for Aria as it celebrates 25 years as an independent retailer and expands with a new outlet over the road on the corner of Upper Street. Onwards and upwards.

COEXISTENCE

288 UPPER STREET N1 2TZ

020 7354 8817

COEXISTENCE.CO.UK

MON-THU 10-6, FRI 10-5

HIGHBURY & ISLINGTON

There's a reason the interior of this Upper Street stalwart reads a bit corporate: for more than 30 years Coexistence has operated for the trade, a point of contact between manufacturers and interior designers and the ho-hum world of office managers. Recently, though, this L-shaped glass warehouse opened to a whole new market of Islingtonian homeowners. And though the premises haven't changed radically, they've gotten slightly homelier. Recently, a pair of decidedly non-corporate 1948 *Rocker* chairs by Race Furniture made it into the front window, upholstered in a lively weatherproof fabric for a garden or conservatory (from £838). And the showroom attendant has evidently been versed in the art of the welcome.

Still, this is the place to get your dining chairs en masse and if you're in the market for a dozen *Metro* chairs by Thomas Sandell for Offecct, for instance. Coexistence stocks literally 100 seating brands, including lesser-knowns like Mark from England, Birdman from Holland and the Basque chair manufacturer Stua. It does a brisk trade in vast dining/boardroom tables and desks. And it operates an in-house exhibition space for partner brands in interesting collaborations.

ESTABLISHED & SONS

5-7 WENLOCK ROAD N1 7SL

020 7608 0990

ESTABLISHEDANDSONS.COM

MON-FRI 9:30-5:30

OLD STREET/ANGEL

When Alasdhair Willis, the former *Wallpaper* magazine publisher, established Established & Sons in 2005, few companies had the wherewithal to invest in contemporary British design in a way that would elevate it onto the footing of the reputable Italian houses. Established hired a roster of Brits who took the twee out of the vernacular local style and added an esoteric, high-spec quality that stood entirely on its own.

Early commissions came from the team of Richard Woods and Sebastian Wrong, Alexander Taylor, and architects like Zaha Hadid and Amanda Levete, who interpreted the common table with outsized scale and personality. But it soon grew to include like-minded Europeans such as the Bouroullec brothers, Sylvain Willenz and Jaime Hayon, whose *Tudor* chair takes British heritage onto an OTT plane.

You'll find choice Established designs across London from Liberty to Mint, but to see them all in one place is to experience awe. That includes getting inside. Find the window stencilled with the company logo, then scan along to the right, where you'll eventually find a barely-marked door, across from the Wenlock Arms. Buzz and an employee will welcome you into the showroom, and give you a knowledgeable tour to boot.

05 ESTORICK COLLECTION

39A CANONBURY SQUARE N1 2AN

020 7704 9522

ESTORICKCOLLECTION.COM

WED–SAT 11–6, SUN 12–5

HIGHBURY & ISLINGTON

After a place has turned 15, is it still permissible to call it a 'find'? In the case of the Estorick, the answer is yes. This lovely bow-windowed Georgian end of terrace has remained charmingly off the beaten path, partly due to its location in residential Canonbury and partly due to its niche content: a collection of Italian art from the Futurist period and beyond.

Assembled by the American writer and art dealer Eric Estorick and his wife Salome over several visits to Italy in the mid-20th century, the collection occupies the upper three floors of this walled townhouse. There are Bocconis, Modiglianis and de Chiricos – artists who get pride of place at Tate Modern and elsewhere – and special exhibitions that span the creative output of modern Italy, from Missoni fashion to fascist propaganda during the reign of Mussolini. Many locals, however, seem content to simply browse the peaceful library (by appointment) and bookshop, or sit out on the terrace with a tiramisu or pizza slice from the café.

06 FANDANGO

2 CROSS STREET N1 2BL

07979 650 805

FANDANGOINTERIORS.CO.UK

WED–SAT 11–6

ESSEX ROAD/HIGHBURY & ISLINGTON/ANGEL

This wedge of a shop has gradually become part of the fabric of Islington – and of most of the renovated terrace houses around Barnsbury and Canonbury. The slight location is less hospitable than an earlier incarnation further up Cross Street, but owners Henrietta Palmer and Jonathan Ellis more than make up for that.

Ellis, when I see him, is visibly proud of his cache of midcentury desks, sunburst mirrors and chrome. He has a knack for accessorising with the neon of the day, along with eccentric ceramics picked up on scouts to Germany, Benelux and beyond. And the unparalleled collection of 1920s glass and midcentury industrial lighting casts a golden glow that makes everything around it appear just right – the magical antidote to the white-on-white Scandi trend.

Design classics do make an appearance, nestled amid anonymous yet characterful gems such as industrial cast-offs, old French café furniture or sturdy school desks. It's worth remembering that they also offer a restoration service, particularly suited to mid-20th century furniture repairs.

As independent boutiques continue to fall like dominoes in the southern reaches of Upper Street, a strong cluster remains in the upper Upper, the youngest of which is Folklore. Here is justification for bricks-and-mortar shopping: a collection of inventive, highly tactile objects in wood and paper, fabrics and knits so natural you can almost smell the rawness.

Folklore is no misnomer; most pieces have a traditional quality, like hand-woven blankets, trophy antlers made of cardboard, and flax potholders. If throwback-chic is your look, there's little chance you'll leave without buying a gift for an old auntie or your next hostess. Only the furniture is priced outside most gift budgets, tables in reclaimed metal and wood in the £2,500 to £3,500 range and the eclectic *High Shore Cabinet*, scrapwood hinged together with handmade hardware for £2,950.

Yes, products may be made from chemical-free materials, crafted from reclaimed wood or infinitely recyclable, yet the eco agenda evident in Folklore's buying criteria thankfully refrains from overtly socking the message to you.

07 FOLKLORE
- 193 UPPER STREET N1 1RQ
- 020 7354 9333
- SHOPFOLKLORE.COM
- TUE-SUN 11-6
- HIGHBURY & ISLINGTON

At the end of the day, Kvadrat is a textile manufacturer. Unless you're a one-percenter who's discovered the line of soft-cell 3D soundproofing wall tiles designed by Ronan and Erwan Bouroullec, you'll be coming here for its rich wool upholstery textiles. But you'll leave inspired beyond the sum of those parts.

In 2009 the Danish manufacturer opened its boundary-pushing London flagship, designed by David Adjaye with help from legendary graphic designer Peter Saville, and it's worth a visit, whatever your personal style. Do make the trip to this post-industrial side street near the City Road Basin. When you buzz in, a shop assistant will lead you down a staircase, past a glass wall in a spectrum of colours, to a lower-level space furnished with nothing but concrete counters.

Or so it seems. The seemingly bare back wall is actually fitted with pull-out kitchen-style cabinets that house all of its fabric collections. The concrete counters come in handy when you've pulled out your choices for closer inspection. They're also great for product launches and Kvadrat's busy calendar of events, during which guests perch on the shallow stairs to absorb the cultural undertakings.

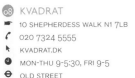

08 KVADRAT
- 10 SHEPHERDESS WALK N1 7LB
- 020 7324 5555
- KVADRAT.DK
- MON-THU 9-5:30, FRI 9-5
- OLD STREET

09 LAGO ISLINGTON

- 36 CROSS STREET N1 2BG
- (020 7359 3950
- ↖ LONDON-ISLINGTON.LAGOSTORE.NET
- ● MON-SAT 9:30-6, SUN 12-5
- ⊖ HIGHBURY & ISLINGTON/ANGEL

The Cross Street branch of Living Space was turning over so much furniture by the Italian brand Lago, it resolved last year to devote itself exclusively to the brand. This was always a hot spot for the austere modular furniture that makes an Islington warren a highly functioning concern. Yet streamlining the concept was a smooth move.

These days when you walk into the erstwhile Living Space, an encyclopaedia of a shop assistant tells you that, across the board, every item can be customised to your specs. Block storage can be wall-mounted, low-slung, configured as a room divider, arranged in stylised designs or transformed into coordinating kitchen cabinetry. Your bed can be appended with any number of shelves, niches or drawers. You can have your wardrobe panelled to match your sofa. Lago has also introduced a live-oak *Wildwood* collection for a 'reclaimed' look you won't have to retrofit into your interior.

10 THE PEANUT VENDOR

- 133 NEWINGTON GREEN ROAD N1 4RA
- (020 7226 5727
- ↖ THEPEANUTVENDOR.CO.UK
- ● TUE-THU 10-7, FRI-SAT 10-6, SUN 12-6
- ⊖ CANONBURY/DALSTON JUNCTION

'Bargain' and 'vintage' have long since lost their ability to exist in the same sentence in London. And yet this hole-in-the-wall in Highbury's furthest reaches manages to buck the trend. Quite literally stuffed to the rafters, with the odd salvaged bench decorating the pavement, the Peanut Vendor's strategy seems to be: sell just enough to be able to close the door at the end of the day.

That said the stuff is honest and well-sourced, ticking a checklist of early- to mid-20th-century British, Danish and French teak and rosewood classics – not by sought-after designers, mind you, but their peers and disciples. Odd tin signage, Bakelite jewellery and ceramic curios give personality to the place, as do the owners, Barny and Becky, whose life's work is market-hopping for quality bargoons.

11 SMUG

- 13 CAMDEN PASSAGE N1 8EA
- 020 7354 0253
- IFEELSMUG.COM
- WED, FRI, SAT 11-6, THU 12-7, SUN 12-5
- ANGEL

They have reason to feel smug here, in their highly covetable snug in Camden Passage with their highly covetable collection of truly lovable graphic homewares. The shop is operated by working designer Lizzie Evans and it shows in her highly informed selection of woolly textiles and stationery. Evans commissions exclusives from some of Britain's most compelling new designer-makers. Ali Miller does a range of illustrated teaware and Matt Pugh riffs on his popular oak and walnut owl figurines. For less than £20, you can bank a hostess gift or welcome another baby to the world. Thornback & Peel does its revival hankies in an exclusive pattern for Smug. You'll convince yourself that no one should be without them, once you see the box set of three.

Vintage furniture items are for sale and, with space here being such a premium, cleverly double as displays for the smaller pieces. Staff are friendly, knowledgeable and passionate, giving Smug a firm footing in the independent retail scene.

12 TWENTYTWENTYONE SHOP

274 UPPER STREET N1 2UA

020 7288 1996

TWENTYTWENTYONE.COM

MON-SAT 10-6, SUN 11-5

HIGHBURY & ISLINGTON

The sun always shines on Twentytwentyone – partly due to its corner location, set back from the road amid low-rise buildings, and partly due to its glass-box construction that draws in natural light no matter what the weather (a major expansion to open up the interior has helped). The conceit is in the name. Twentytwentyone is a haven for enduring 20th-century design that keeps on top of the latest product developments. And even though it first popped up before the 21st century had even begun (1996), it has always delivered.

And what it delivers is dreams. Any chair you've ever coveted will likely be in stock, propped up in a niche in the back surrounded by a halo of light. All those life-changing storage solutions are here, adorned with goodies for the luckiest of children. Meanwhile, the window is where new dreams are made: a reissued Saarinen armchair, reupholstered in fresh citrus-coloured wool, or the ideal contemporary dining table from Another Country.

It all comes at a cost, naturally – unless you've come to simply bask in it all. Which in itself can be the stuff of dreams.

13 *Molecular mixology*

The master of cocktails Tony Conigliaro serves his cleverly masterminded drinks in this tiny 'Bar With No Name' down a backstreet in Islington. Possibly the finest cocktails in London served in a dark and sultry room. Booking a table is a must.

69 COLEBROOKE ROW 69 COLEBROOKE ROW N1 8AA
07540 528 593 | 69COLEBROOKEROW.COM

14 *Fish & chips*

The chef is ex-Ivy, great, simple cooking with good prices. London Particular Fritters are addictive (ham hock/pea), crisp, light battered fish, lobster roll and shrimp burger. Distressed interior, seafood bar, and take-away service.

THE FISH & CHIP SHOP 189 UPPER STREET N1 1RQ
020 3227 0979 | THEFISHANDCHIPSHOP.UK.COM

15 *Theatrical drinking*

A three-story 'multi-sensory experimental pleasure palace' in Islington's oldest Victorian music hall. With endless varied rooms, this is more theatre than bar and restaurant. Experimental cocktails and guest chefs.

HOUSE OF WOLF [PICTURED] 181 UPPER STREET N1 1RQ
020 7288 1470 | HOUSEOFWOLF.CO.UK

16 *Pie, mash n' liquor*

Proper, traditional working man's pie n' mash shop with marble tables, wooden benches and tiled walls. Single or double pies with mash and liquor (parsley sauce) or try the jellied eels. All accompanied by a cuppa.

L MANZE 74 CHAPEL MARKET N1 9ER
020 7837 5270

17 *Taste explosions*

Ottolenghi's flagship of tantalising food displays. Inventive, flavoursome dishes made from top-quality ingredients to eat in or take away. Sleek, white interior that makes the colourful food stand out. Packed at weekends, can reserve for dinner.

OTTOLENGHI 287 UPPER STREET N1 2TZ
020 7288 1454 | OTTOLENGHI.CO.UK

18 Handmade truffles

Fine artisan chocolatier on picturesque pedestrian walk. Decadent chocolates made by hand on site each day. Thick and very chocolaty hot chocolate. Cult chocolate has to be the Marmite truffle.

PAUL A YOUNG CHOCOLATES 33 CAMDEN PASSAGE N1 8EA
020 7424 5750 | PAULAYOUNG.CO.UK

19 Canalside brunch

Soulful, small-scale canalside café decidedly off the beaten track. Open during the day, only in warmer months. Serves flavourful top-quality café favourites and great coffee. Peaceful treasure in London.

TOWPATH CAFÉ 42 DE BEAUVOIR CRESCENT N1 5SB
020 7254 7606

20 Galician tapas

Neighbourhood restaurant on two floors serving exceptional daily-changing tapas and Spanish wines. Full of vintage and antique chairs, tables, chandeliers, all for sale. Tables are squeezed in tightly, but it creates a fun atmosphere.

TRANGALLAN 61 NEWINGTON GREEN N16 9PX
020 7359 4988 | TRANGALLAN.COM

21 Rustic Italian

Excellent local that is hugely popular. Warm, intimate interior serving up robust Italian dishes packed with flavour. Superb wine list and further dining room and bar in the basement.

TRULLO 300-302 ST PAUL'S ROAD N1 2LH
020 7226 2733 | TRULLORESTAURANT.COM

PROVENENCE *continued from p.125*

it is made of. We're selling premium products so people expect them to have a proper lifespan and trust that they've come from well-sourced origins.

SHERIDAN COAKLEY

We try hard to ask where everything is made because people are interested in it, but surprisingly, producers are not obliged to tell you. Now on our website, if we know where a product is from, we will put it on there.

MAGNUS ENGLUND

It's interesting to look at the food industry; we want to know what we're putting in our mouths, so we also start questioning where other products in our lives come from.

LINA KANAFANI

Over time, China will be able to produce to a very high quality and in smaller quantities so I don't think we'll have this debate in the future.

RHONDA DRAKEFORD

I still think that a lot of people are more bothered about the price. In our niche, we're lucky that we deal with customers that do seem to care.

MAX FRASER

What about own-brand ranges?

MAGNUS ENGLUND

We've been surprised at how successful it has been to introduce our own products. We are now one of the biggest suppliers to ourselves! The staff really takes it on board and they feel extra pride when they sell something, and we've also managed to manufacture some of our pieces in the UK.

MAX FRASER

Presumably there's a higher up-front risk but the margins are better?

MAGNUS ENGLUND

I wouldn't say significantly better, but they are better. We are trying to aim for an accessible basic product with a medium price.

SHERIDAN COAKLEY

It's misleading if you think that you'll make a higher margin, because you have to invest in developing your own products. Of course, if you wholesale them, there are other risks involved. It's about building what you're trying to do rather than just making higher margins.

INTERNET SELLING

MAX FRASER

What about designers or brands – your suppliers – selling directly to customers via mono-brand stores and/or their own websites?

RHONDA DRAKEFORD

We've definitely had to have a word with some of our suppliers when they were selling their products for a lower price on their own websites.

LINA KANAFANI

If you're in control of your product as the producer, then the internet is perfect because it allows you to communicate your profile around the world – to market and promote yourself. But to be in the middle, it's much harder.

MAX FRASER

Lina, I remember you talking about removing the product and supplier name from the items you sell so that customers don't hunt for the same product elsewhere.

LINA KANAFANI

True. This 'search ability' is happening and to the advantage of the consumer, definitely. They have more knowledge available now and I know that we're not going to be able to stop them. We should embrace it, but at the same time I feel like it does affect my business and, up to now, in a negative way.

JAMES MAIR

Websites are crucial to what we all do and you have to maximise what you're doing through your website. One shouldn't just offer a shopping list but should explain your history, your story, your after-care service etc. The internet can reinforce your assets rather than detract and you just have to welcome it.

SHERIDAN COAKLEY

We are in a very niche market and the benefit

Continued p.166

'DRAWING LETS YOU EXPRESS THINGS IN A DIFFERENT WAY. YOU CAN BE SAD OR YOU CAN BE ROMANTIC. YOU CAN BE AN IDIOT. ANYTHING CAN WORK IN A DRAWING'

RONAN BOUROULLEC

disegnodaily.com

Shoreditch
& Brick Lane

E.1

E2

E.C.2

N.I

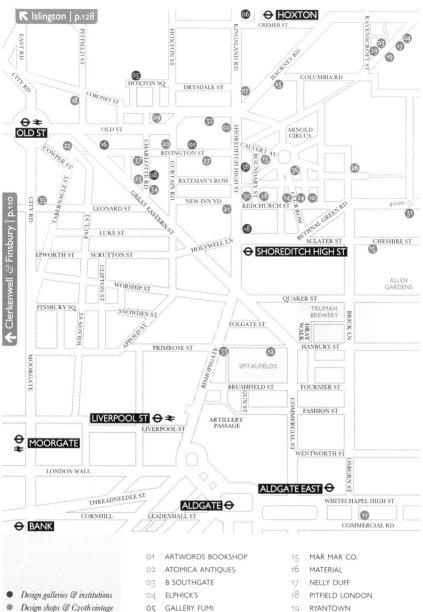

Islington | p.128

HOXTON

Clerkenwell & Finsbury | p.110

OLD ST

SHOREDITCH HIGH ST

LIVERPOOL ST

MOORGATE

ALDGATE EAST

ALDGATE

BANK

- Design galleries & institutions
- Design shops & C20th vintage
- Design bookshops

- Eat & drink (pp.164-165)

01	ARTWORDS BOOKSHOP	15	MAR MAR CO.
02	ATOMICA ANTIQUES	16	MATERIAL
03	B SOUTHGATE	17	NELLY DUFF
04	ELPHICK'S	18	PITFIELD LONDON
05	GALLERY FUMI	19	RYANTOWN
06	GEFFRYE MUSEUM	20	SCP EAST
07	JASPER MORRISON SHOP	21	SQUINT
08	KEMISTRY GALLERY	22	TOKYOBIKE
09	KK OUTLET	23	TORD BOONTJE
10	LABOUR AND WAIT	24	TRACEY NEULS
11	LIGNE ROSET CITY	25	TWO COLUMBIA ROAD
12	THE LOLLIPOP SHOPPE	26	UNTO THIS LAST
13	LUNA & CURIOUS	27	YCN
14	MAISON TROIS GARÇONS		

Street*wise*

When did you move to this street?
In 2010 when we opened menswear store Hostem.

What originally attracted you to it?
We were attracted to the rough and tumble of the street.
Development was minimal at the time and only Shoreditch
House and the Boundary Hotel had recently opened. A feeling of
authenticity pervaded this corner of East London. The street reeked
of history, but it was certainly a risk as it appeared so rundown
and nothing like it is today. The street is one big building site at the
moment and is essentially in a profound state of flux.

**How has this shopping thoroughfare changed
since you've been here?**
Some of the galleries have moved out, but we have gained the likes
of Allpress for coffee, Labour & Wait utility store, and food from the
inimitable Les Trois Garcons. Some retail has been welcome, but
equally, other developments have highlighted the downside of all
the attention the street has received since 2010.

What does the street offer the community that is unique?
Ultimately the street is only as strong as its inhabitants. The artistic,
creative core is still intact and people, cliched as it may sound,
genuinely look out for each other. This becomes really apparent
when larger developments are proposed which provoke some
debate. Some of the historical elements to the street are truly
unique, from being on the fringes of Britain's first social housing
scheme, the Boundary Estate, built in the 19th century, to the fact
that one of the oldest riflemakers in the country, Watson Brothers,
is still in-situ and going strong.

Tell us about some of your neighbouring hotspots?
Allpress for caffeine, Leila's for breakfast and provisions, Rochelle
Canteen for lunch, and Brawn for dinner.

**What has recently changed on neighbouring roads that
has alarmed you?**
Unfortunately, I don't feel that Boxpark has benefited the area.
The retail, cultural and entertainment mix needs to be much better
thought through on many of the local streets in general.

If you could change one thing on the street, what would it be?
If we could just divert some of the weekend's socially inspired
invaders, the area would shine a little more brightly!

James Brown
Hostem

41-43 REDCHURCH STREET E2 7DJ
020 7739 9733 HOSTEM.CO.UK

REDCHURCH STREET

01 ARTWORDS BOOKSHOP

- 69 RIVINGTON STREET EC2A 3AY
- 020 7729 2000
- ARTWORDS.CO.UK
- MON-FRI 10.30-7, SAT 11-7
- OLD STREET/HOXTON/SHOREDITCH HIGH STREET

Artwords Bookshop is all aflurry during the lunch hour, when rail-thin Shoreditch creatives nourish themselves with weighty tomes on contemporary German photorealists of the 1970s or peek furtively at photo-tributes to Jeff Koons. Its speciality is contemporary art and design, which extends to graphic novels, videos, selected magazines and special editions: fairly specialised stuff, making a sojourn here feels like an edifying stroll through a gallery. Not surprisingly, it has the cachet of a gallery; authors and artists often hold events and signings here, packing the stark white space to capacity.

02 ATOMICA ANTIQUES

- 125 SHOREDITCH HIGH STREET E1 6JE
- 020 7739 5923
- ATOMICA.ME.UK
- TUE-SUN, 11.30-5.30
- SHOREDITCH HIGH STREET

It has the aura of one of those piled-to-the-rafters antiques dealers of yore, except that the stock is exceptionally well considered, tailored to this neighbourhood of design-schooled sophisticates. And literally so: of the rich cache of Danish oak armchairs and love seats, the ones with damaged upholstery have been refitted with Paul Smith striped tailoring, repurposed burlap or even lumberjack wool check. The selection of lighting has been tightly curated to include a small selection of Hala desk lamps from Holland and Italian pendants. Storage from defunct apothecaries or soda shops has a sense of humour – not unlike eclectica, such as a pair of leg braces from the turn of the 20th century.

- 4 THE COURTYARD, EZRA STREET E2 7RH
- 07905 960792
- BSOUTHGATE.CO.UK
- SUN 9-3
- HOXTON

You know you're getting close to Columbia Road's Sunday flower market when you start seeing shoppers strolling away lugging pots of herbs, bamboo and lavender. What you may not notice are the vans hauling substantial chrome display units and aged leather club chairs off site at Ben Southgate's courtyard showroom.

But people have been, for years. It may be debatable whether Southgate came first or the trend for interiors seemingly lifted off the set of a 1950s Hollywood noir, but that's neither here nor there. Southgate's early-20th-century stock is indisputably true to the look, with an integrity that's not inevitable in London. And the locals have noticed.

Hours are frustratingly infrequent – Sundays only, while the market is in full swing. Southgate spends the rest of his week in his East Sussex workshops restoring worn leather and shattered oak joinery, fixing the ring on a vintage globe or tightening the label plates on a Wellington chest. When it makes it to market, you know it's been approved from the top.

- 160 COLUMBIA ROAD E2 7RG
- 020 7033 7891
- ELPHICKSSHOP.COM
- SAT 12-5, SUN 9-4
- HOXTON

Columbia Road is a bit of a non-entity on weekdays, but come Saturday and especially Sunday, when the morning flower market and attendant buskers give this enclave the feeling of Portobello, the vibrant throng of boutiques throws open its doors and the punters arrive to see what all the fuss is about. Elphick's, toward the far end of the strip, has become something of an anchor in recent years, for its graphic pop art – ready framed, if you can spare the extra cash – and arty stationery.

Sharon Elphick's gallery was hard won, after a decade showing her whimsical collage art at galleries and fairs from here to Tokyo. With Elphick's she seems to have pegged the neighbourhood zeitgeist, showing not only her own vibrant pastiches but those of peers like East End graphic artist James Brown and the folky Lisa Jones and Audrey Jeanne. Both the salt-of-the-earth market-goers and the new crop of homeowners who have played a role in the area's gentrification go in for the crisp silhouettes in vivid colours she prudently curates – a sort of contemporary folk that stops short of being twee. Other galleries have imitated her magic formula but fall short.

 GALLERY FUMI

16 HOXTON SQUARE N1 6NT

020 7490 2366

GALLERYFUMI.COM

APPOINTMENT ONLY

HOXTON/OLD STREET

Collectible design has made strides over the past decade, engendering trade fairs like the Design Miami/Basel series, Design Days Dubai and PAD, the Paris show in which Fumi has taken part since 2008. Still the industry largely operates behind salon doors à la Gertrude Stein in 1920s Paris. Now that it has shuttered its space in Tabernacle Street, Fumi's business has returned to this parlour on a fourth floor overlooking Hoxton Square. Despite the killer view, you might feel as if you've fallen down the rabbit hole here, in among urns of Jesmonite that look like marble, rubber vases that appear liquid, Dentalium shells that feel vaguely threatening.

Do come, though. Ring ahead from your perch in Hoxton Square and navigate the (Wonderland-style) signposts to this vaulted reception. Valerio Capo or Sam Pratt, directors since the 2008 launch, will lead you past the wall of four-metre glass doors to the ceiling-high hand-carved plywood dividing screen, by Zoe Ouvrier; CoWorks' waxed-copper bowls; or Faye Toogood's resin cube with suspended oil sphere (don't sit on it lest you scratch it with a trendy zipper). Their enthusiasm, though infectious, is simply a reflection of the art – more impressive for its usefulness. It will extend to you, this enthusiasm. Soak it all up.

 GEFFRYE MUSEUM

136 KINGSLAND ROAD E2 8EA

020 7739 9893

GEFFRYE-MUSEUM.ORG.UK

TUE–SAT 10–5, SUN 12–5

HOXTON/OLD STREET

In London you often find the dearest treasures when you walk a few blocks out of your way. Case in point: the Geffrye Museum, housed in a block of 18th-century almshouses with a generous swath of manicured green out front and mazes of period gardens in back, chronologically arranged to complement the rooms inside.

Poking around the herbs or basking on the lawns while counting the white mullioned windows is as good a way to spend an afternoon as any. And yet the interior is the Geffrye's raison d'etre: a collection of quintessential English rooms arranged in a timeline from 1600 to the present. The old corridors bypass period bedrooms and salons accompanied by anecdotal text and an interactive quiz for the kids.

At its centre, the home opens up into a library and reading room overlooking the rose gardens, before tapering off again for more displays. A new wing incorporates a rotunda with an exhibition of 20th-century furnishings, plus a gift shop, event hall, basement gallery and hands-on rooms for children. The restaurant, serving lunches and tea, occupies a contemporary conservatory with views of the award-winning walled herb garden.

07 JASPER MORRISON SHOP

24B KINGSLAND ROAD E2 8DA

N/A

JASPERMORRISON.COM

MON-FRI 11-5

HOXTON/OLD STREET

Don't be intimidated by the buzz-only entrance and the voice emanating from the intercom – you are most welcome here. This snug cube of a shop in the courtyard of designer Jasper Morrison's London studio is like a living encyclopaedia of his product portfolio. Here are the *Glo-Ball* pendants for Flos. There is the steel tableware for Alessi and the bins for Magis. Not forgetting the cork stools for Vitra.

Morrison is one of the UK's – nay the world's – most influential industrial designers, renowned for his talent for revitalising basic, functional products in the purest form possible, tickled with wit if not whimsy. But his celebrity hardly means his smooth, simple solutions for everyday life are unaffordable for those who would most appreciate them. Even his canvas and suede shoes for Camper are a steal at £75.

Morrison's cordless phones for Punkt (£155) are a clear draw, as is the library in the back room, including several seminal design paperbacks from the 1950s to the present day, displayed modestly on one wall. But Morrison also highlights designs from other 'function over form' designers and manufacturers, like Alessi's citrus juicer, and the iconic Giannina espresso maker.

That said, no emphasis is put on designer name or brand here. Only the immaculate label-free product displays guide your decision making, supported by the knowledge and expertise of the friendly shop assistant should you need it.

Graphic design has lately crept into the art-world vernacular – particularly in East London, where the bulk of creative agencies do their arresting print and multimedia work. Slowly, illustrators and printmakers with a powerful voice and a knack for geometry and typography in contemporary colour palettes are beginning to show their work in a gallery setting. And Kemistry on Charlotte Road, a major thoroughfare on the Shoreditch creative map, is one of the places to show.

One of very few independent galleries devoted to graphic artists, past and present, Kemistry gets cred for its tight professional relationship with Anthony Burrill, the godfather of contemporary graphic art in the UK and creator of the 'Work hard and be nice to people' meme – not to mention a pivotal poster series for the London Underground. Recently it exhibited a series of prints and short films by the London-based French artist Malika Farve, and a round-up of projects, posters and models by the Norwegian design studio Yokoland.

08 KEMISTRY GALLERY

- 43 CHARLOTTE ROAD EC2A 3PD
- 020 7729 3636
- KEMISTRYGALLERY.CO.UK
- MON–SAT 10-6
- OLD STREET/SHOREDITCH HIGH STREET

09 KK OUTLET

- 42 HOXTON SQUARE N1 6PB
- 020 7033 7680
- KKOUTLET.COM
- MON–FRI 9-6, SAT 12-5
- HOXTON/OLD STREET

If you were a hot, sassy creative agency with an empty storefront on hip Hoxton Square, what would you do with it? The answer is still debatable, if the passers-by peering in the front window and scratching their heads are anything to go by. And that's half the appeal of this place.

KK – a division of KesselsKramer, the Amsterdam-based multichannel communications agency – reinvents the ground-floor gallery-bookshop on a monthly basis. One month may see a photo exhibition featuring images from the Shit London website, ahead of its annual awards ceremony. Another may feature memorial china plates inspired by the Royal Wedding. There is always a collection of thematic crafts to purchase as souvenirs or novelty gifts, and a decent library of art and design tomes, often with a tongue-in-cheek slant.

Shopping in Shoreditch and Spitalfields can sometimes seem like drifting back into the *Belle Epoque*, the signs written in Art Nouveau cursive, the simple, functional wares wrapped in brown paper. You can thank Labour and Wait, largely, for this development – or should I say retrogression. More than a dozen years ago it popped up on nearby Cheshire Street selling waxed aprons, feather dusters and egg beaters, enduring products that flew in the face of New Millennium consumerism.

The General Store model endured and Labour and Wait grew into a former pub on burgeoning Redchurch Street just as the fashion for sturdy, reliable dry goods was reaching the mainstream. In the process it's played a part in keeping some long-established European manufacturers in the business of, say, enamelware, aluminium dustpans and Kreide dustless chalk. You might pay £9 for a steel can opener from France after a kind, moustachioed shop assistant wows you with a demo – and yes, a £3 supermarket model would do the job in a pinch. But said can opener will blow your mind – and likely still be around when your unborn children move into their first flat.

11 LIGNE ROSET CITY

37-39 COMMERCIAL ROAD E1 1LF

020 7426 9670

LIGNE-ROSET-CITY.CO.UK

MON-SAT 10-6, THU 10-7, SUN 12-5

ALDGATE EAST

It's wholesale heaven out here on the boundary between creative London and the old garment district – an awkward locale for the typical (well-heeled, West London) Ligne Roset customer, perhaps, but perfect for backing in a moving van. And there's plenty at this large London location that you'll want to truck over to yours. The stalwart French manufacturer may still stock some of the same styles that secured it a place in the furniture canon years ago, but a brilliant and always modern range of vibrant suede, velvet and wool upholsteries – plus a growing roster of accessories – keeps it relevant. Though you really have to see it up close to believe it.

In fact, just sit. That £3,000 *Pumpkin* sofa by Pierre Paulin, those *Confluences* seats by Philippe Nigro or the modular *Nomade-Express* by Didier Gomez may be just out of your budget, but your bottom will confirm what you already know: it'll last a lifetime. Paulin's 1955 *Archi* chairs have never looked more modern than in citrus wool alongside a *Picnic* table by GamFratesi or a *Gamba* pedestal table by Sam Baron. They get a lot of play these days at LR, along with Dögg & Arnved's fabulously tiki *Fifty* armchair and the Bouroullec brothers' conceptual oeuvre – pieces of interactive art that will pay dividends in pleasure if you can afford the outlay.

MAYUHANA

Inspired by the classic Japanese ricespool lanterns and the spun fibres of a butterfly cocoon, soft, warm light, glows from deep within these delicate, glass fibre lamps. The Mayuhana collection is designed by the Japanese star architect, Toyo Ito, features a range of exquisite, Japanese handmade pendants, floor and table lamps, which makes this a very versatile collection of decorative lighting.

GATEWAY JAPAN

12 THE LOLLIPOP SHOPPE

🏠 10 LAMB STREET E1 6EA

📞 020 7655 4540

🔗 THELOLLIPOPSHOPPE.CO.UK

🕐 MON-SAT 10-6, SUN 11-5

🚇 LIVERPOOL STREET/SHOREDITCH HIGH STREET

Not everyone was thrilled when gritty, student-led Spitalfields Market got a makeover by the neighbourhood regeneration folks, along with a few new high-street tenants to pay down the investment. But the spruce-up doesn't seem to have done much to reduce the market's cachet. And one of the positive legacies has been an influx of interesting shops: relatively high rent, but with the grass-roots ethos Spitalfields has always espoused. The Lollipop Shoppe is the finest of the lot.

Owners Marco and Siobhan Di Rienzo manage to fit a comprehensive library of design classics into the bijou setting. To one side, in a series of niches, is a cross section of furnishings by greats like Eames, Aalto and Vitra, plus British brands Ercol and Tom Dixon. Into the rest is shoehorned a staggering collection of goodies for the eyes (elegant table lamps from Muuto and Fritz Hansen), the mind (architectural models of British icons and wind-up radios by Lexon), the soul (Malin + Goetz toiletries), and the kids (dolls by Studio Matryoshka and Alexander Girard).

All this is slipped stylishly into the heritage building, the brickwork peeking out in places between displays, seamlessly straddling the Spitalfields of old and new.

Luna & Curious's western flank hosts pop-up events, the most recent of which was a throwback barber doing straight-razor shaves and hipster beards. Meanwhile, the main showroom rather touchingly displays art, craft and fashion from the neighbourhood ateliers, where creatives toy with lighting, weave feathers into audacious millinery and print stationery by hand.

The store is owned and run by Kaoru Parry, Polly George and Rheanna Lingham, who have cultivated a space that is as much gallery as shop, tending toward surreal, Wonderland-style displays that leap from the white walls. Fashion junkies will claim this place for their own; the inventive jewellery and irreverent colour-block tights are style coups. But Luna's strong suit is its singular collection of porcelain. Polly George's all-white tabletop ceramics with butterfly appliqués are feats of the kiln. Table settings by We Love Kaoru are equally loveable: classic shapes trimmed in gold with subversive patterns, like the Rorschach-inspired *Ink Blot* series of plates and mugs. Kaoru Parry, the mind behind the label, will warn you they're not suitable for dishwashing and point you instead toward Yas-Ming's *Moo* cups with animal-head handles.

13 LUNA & CURIOUS
- 24-26 CALVERT AVENUE E2 7JP
- 020 3222 0034
- LUNAANDCURIOUS.COM
- MON-SAT 11-6, SUN 11-5
- HOXTON/SHOREDITCH HIGH STREET

Next time you duck past a mounted stag's head before nestling into a Louis XVI settee, remember who got you there. Trois Garçons – the shop, then the restaurant, the lounge and finally this 'lifestyle' café – pioneered the neo Baroque-Méribel chalet look that's been doing the rounds in Shoreditch for a decade. For four years this L-shaped corner shop flogged gilded mirrors, tarnished candelabras and bombastic lighting the owners picked up at markets across Western Europe, all with that intrinsic TG glamour.

Now, to get more bang for their rising rent, owners Hassan Abdullah, Michel Lasserre and Stefan Karlson have pushed the shop wares against the walls and adapted the open floor into a restaurant with Portuguese tables and 1960s school chairs (available for purchase). The elaborate mirrors and brass bar carts are still here, along with the Louis silhouettes, but these days, I am told, the upholsteries are updated and the silver polished. The customers prefer it that way.

Likewise, there's new stuff in the corners: cushions printed with King Charles spaniels, 'Murano effect' mirrors and John Moncrieff's *Memory Balloon* ceiling lights. It's all loads of fun. And now you can mull it over with a slice of quiche (served with a smile) and some of London's finest people-watching.

14 MAISON TROIS GARÇONS
- 45 REDCHURCH STREET E2 7DJ
- 020 3370 7761
- LESTROISGARCONS.COM/SHOP
- MON-FRI 8-7, SAT-SUN 9-7
- SHOREDITCH HIGH STREET

15 MAR MAR CO.

🚩 16 CHESHIRE STREET E2 6EH

📞 020 7729 1494

🔗 MARMARCO.COM

🕐 THU-FRI & SUN 11-5, SAT 12-5

⊖ SHOREDITCH HIGH STREET

For every gritty high street in London there's a Cheshire Street, a peaceful shopping respite from the crowds and congestion of the main thoroughfare – in this case, Brick Lane. The Cheshire Street merchants are a tight community of independent, artisanal, vintage-lovers, and Mar Mar Co is their anchor. Gallery-like in its spare displays and clean, light-strewn interior, it is loved internationally for its tightly curated selection of toys, gifts and tableware made in the UK and Northern Europe.

For these products, as for the interior, the beauty is in the simplicity, like a *Trook* coat hook crafted from natural tree cuttings (for their trouble, the scavenger-designers get £7 to £12), or a spatula with a few clever holes punched through to help you strain your pasta. There's always a collection of nesting dolls on display, whimsically hand-painted like owls or zoo animals, and tea towels that will have you reaching for your wallet.

16 MATERIAL

🚩 3 RIVINGTON STREET EC2A 3DT

📞 020 7739 1900

🔗 WWW.MATERIALMATERIAL.COM

🕐 MON-FRI 11-7, SAT 11-6

⊖ OLD STREET

With Charing Cross increasingly unreliable for books of an artistic bent, someone had to pick up the slack. Enter Joseph Gimlik and Lucy Payne who launched this 'concept bookshop' as a middle ground between the dusty antiquarians and the grandiose £250-a-tome boutiques. They support designers and artists of all styles, from twee and painterly to Saul Bass-bold at prices that are affordable even to Shoreditch interns.

Material is determined to keep you stocking your shelves with actual reading material, and they keep a stock of 'testers' to lure you in to the books of the moment. But there's also a good selection of limited-edition prints, as well as gifts and stationery – the bread and butter of the modern bookstore.

Students of Cockney rhyming slang can trace the name of this gallery back to 'life', and in the process gain some perspective on the gallery's philosophy. The artists whose original and limited-edition art gets an airing here come from all over the world, but the overarching theme is the street style and the tattoo'd aesthetic born right here in the lifeblood of East London.

Few galleries, if any, have so elevated street art to fine art like Nelly. The gallery makes you think in collector's terms about drip-flawed graffiti and bathroom-wall scrawl, encouraging its roster of artists to more complex techniques and more profound themes. Artists who started here have gone on to contribute to exhibitions at Somerset House, the MoMA and the V&A. Ben Eine, possibly the best known of the lot, has garnered recognition for his limited-edition alphabet poster as well as setting world records for screen printing. Recently you could buy one of 37 signed Eine *Grey Faded Oranges on Red* posters for £525 and rest assured you would one day hold a collector's item.

17 NELLY DUFF
- 156 COLUMBIA ROAD E2 7RG
- 020 7033 9683
- NELLYDUFF.COM
- SAT 12-4, SUN 9-3
- HOXTON

Pitfield seems so out of place here, between hipster Hoxton Square and that dastardly Old Street roundabout. In a good way, of course. Part Helsinki chic, part Palm Beach, it's like a faraway haven of Pop Art fabrics, Deco-style room dividers and insane orange leather armchairs from the 1960s. Okay, so the staff seem slightly harassed and practically send you reeling as they rush past without saying hello, but not every day can be yours, and when pressed they will rather pleasantly tell you the provenance of the magnificent leather-topped table and matching chairs that would not be out of place at a top West London dealer (Mexico, 1970s, £1,200).

A tea shop with brownies, meringues and free-range chicken pies occupies the north end of the shop – 'an extension of the Pitfield brand', its literature says. What truly distinguishes Pitfield, though, is its roster of exhibitions by independent designers of all walks, from the Helsinki (Klaus Haapaniemi) to the Palm Beach (Jade Jagger). That and Pitfield's obvious respect for interesting pottery by Camille Flammarion and Iittala.

18 PITFIELD LONDON
- 31-35 PITFIELD STREET N1 6HB
- 020 7490 6852
- PITFIELDLONDON.COM
- DAILY 11-7
- HOXTON

19 RYANTOWN

126 COLUMBIA ROAD E2 7RG

020 7613 1510

MISTERROB.CO.UK

SAT 12-6, SUN 10-4

HOXTON

His aesthetic has so distinctively encapsulated London's current craving for the handmade that it's hard to imagine a world without Rob Ryan's paper-cut masterworks. Sure, we had late-career Matisse and the ethereal narratives of Marc Chagall, but Ryan was instrumental in leading a generation back to that naiveté after nearly a century of canny modernist and postmod progress.

These days you can barely browse for Ryanesque greeting cards, children's books and jaunty posters. But the genuine article is here (and on Ryan's website). This five-year-old shop, on the design strip that Columbia Road has become since the local creative tribes calculated a viable living catering to the Sunday market hordes, is aptly named. This is where the artist's cast of cut-out characters comes to roost in uplifting scenes right out of Hans Christian Andersen or Grimm.

Ryan's true craft is his artwork, expertly carved out into positive or negative space as if by a laser in his studio around the corner. He's not above greeting cards or coffee mugs or wall stickers – he practically invented the genre. And his limited-edition prints are justifiably popular. But it's become the ultimate romantic gesture around these parts to commission your own personal Ryan to hang over your four-poster.

20 SCP EAST

135 CURTAIN ROAD EC2A 3BX

020 7739 1869

SCP.CO.UK

MON–SAT 9.30–6, SUN 11–5

OLD STREET

You'd think Sheridan Coakley had done enough, making contemporary British design desirable to the British; helping build careers for local luminaries like Matthew Hilton, Jasper Morrison and Donna Wilson; sustaining a British manufacturing brand; and reviving a forgotten corner of East London. He manages to keep a helpful and informative staff too, at this flagship store in Shoreditch.

Coakley's story has become London lore: how he braved these downtrodden streets in the 1980s to provide a showcase for honest home-grown craftsmen and start a movement that valued simple, functional furnishings built to last. His fabrics are still spun in Yorkshire, his ceramics thrown in Stoke-on-Trent, his furniture upholstered in Norfolk. But his early contributors (can you even remember a time before Terence Woodgate and Tom Dixon?) are now household names the world over.

Downstairs you can comb the tables for hours, flipping through books, fingering cushions and inspecting pottery. Upstairs are the big-ticket items – vast, inviting wood-frame sofas with quality upholstery – and some more affordable children's and occasional furnishings. Kay + Stemmer's impossibly smooth wall-mounted shelving is surprisingly affordable in the low three-digits. It's manufactured by scp, along with Donna Wilson's range, which steals the scene with its distinctive prints and fresh palette.

21 SQUINT

🡒 178 SHOREDITCH HIGH STREET E1 6HU

☎ 020 7739 9275

🡖 SQUINTLIMITED.COM

🕐 MON-FRI 10-6, SUN 1-5

⊖ SHOREDITCH HIGH STREET

Squint's prominent position on Shoreditch High Street is brilliant for sticking it to beige-lovers heading down into the City. It's the retail equivalent of a person who refuses to mince words, a champion of exuberant decoration that sets itself apart from the bleak grey environment.

Lisa Whatmough, who developed this play on tradition about a decade ago and has since stayed true to her signature style, has moved the bar for Brits who crave a more Baroque silhouette to their furniture – and a little more oomph to their upholstery. You can see her influence everywhere now, from the in-vogue velvet upholsteries to the return to flocking and renewed appreciation for the Chesterfield.

Among fans of that look, Squint is the be-all. Whatmough employs long-established British craftsmen to recreate classic styles – her famous tallboys, birdcage tables, Queen Anne mirrors, Chippendale loveseats, even midcentury gems like the *Egg* chair. Then she goes at them with her patchwork of chinoiserie, ticking and bold floral fabrics. Bespoke customers can choose from the 'hotter' or 'cooler' portfolios and choose a dominant hue around which Whatmough will work. Or, if you love her traditional technique but aren't sure about the Mad Hatter aesthetic, you can rein her in for a simple upholstery job.

22 TOKYOBIKE

🡒 87-89 TABERNACLE STREET EC2A 4BA

☎ 020 7251 6842

🡖 TOKYOBIKE.CO.UK

🕐 TUE-SAT 11-7, SUN 12-5

⊖ OLD STREET

For a shop that prides itself on its small stature and indie status, there sure was a lot of fanfare when tokyobike opened in 2012. The design set came with a trail of paparazzi for the niche manufacturer that champions comfort over speed. This is the brand that stocks its wheels at designer Piet Hein Eek's studio in Eindhoven, and that commissioned artists like Tom Pearson and Alex Daw to design one-off cycles as an opening lure. A tokyobike is a comfortable ride, but it's also seriously chic.

As if to drive home the point, the Shoreditch showroom has the reclaimed floors and white walls of a gallery, with slender cycles in candy colours around the perimeter and low displays of Japanese- and British-designed homewares directing the flow – like a grass-roots Muji. The clean-lined, back-to-basics tableware comes courtesy of Momosan, which recently opened its own showroom at 15a Kingsland Road.

Tokyobike staff are Japanese imports too, bike buffs of the smartly dressed sort you rarely see in the London shops. The best argument we've seen yet not to buy local.

After years' designing some of the most sought-after merchandise for retail outlets like Habitat, Tord Boontje rightly resolved to get in on the action. He opened his loft-showroom in 2012 and immediately launched the basement space as a gallery for collaborations with designers big (Swarovski) and small (Tracey Neuls). Yet his *Garland* lights, created for Habitat more than 10 years ago, and their successors *Icarus* and *Midsummer* will always be the top sellers on this well trodden stretch of Charlotte Road.

Boontje leaves no home accessory undesigned, however. Each season brings a new range of glassware or tableware, collaborations with Dartington Crystal, jewellery, and even T-shirts. His stationery and table mats are laser cut with the precision and care of his famous *Garland* lights. But if you'd rather let your partner do the shopping, no one will bat an eye if you take a load off in Boontje's giant chameleon-shaped *Shadowy* lounge chair for Moroso (and you can buy that, too).

23 TORD BOONTJE SHOP

- 23 CHARLOTTE ROAD EC2A 3PB
- 020 7717 5398
- SHOP.TORDBOONTJE.COM
- TUE–SAT 11–6, SUN 12–5
- OLD STREET

The Canadian cobbler might have had a fallback career as a designer, for all the effort she puts into her boutiques. Neuls has always dressed her stores like little homes (you'll find the Marylebone location on p.059), with delicate wood cast-offs and vast contemporary seating gleaned over years. The hefty wool-upholstered armchair in the corner she brought on the plane with her from British Columbia. The neon-sided *M-Bench* in the window is by designer Jennifer Newman.

Neuls, a regular at Clerkenwell Design Week and the London Design Festival, and a favourite collaborator of furniture people like Retrouvius, Moroso and Tord Boontje, has always been into eye-popping colour. The neon threading with which she dangles her sculptural footwear from the shop ceiling is considered classic. Finally the styles (both fashion and furniture) are catching up with her. Stop by on a quiet weekday (weekends are bustling here) and get a load of her designs, hanging so you can view them from all angles, like an architectural object. You'll likely end up in that armchair talking shop with a well-shod manager and spotting like-minded pedestrians on the pavements outside.

24 TRACEY NEULS

- 73 REDCHURCH STREET E2 7DJ
- 020 7018 0872
- TRACEYNEULS.COM
- WED–SUN 11–6
- SHOREDITCH HIGH STREET

Like the trusty mechanic you know will always sort you out at a fair price, Keith Roberts is a rare breed in retail: engaged, hyper-knowledgeable and fair. His lifeblood is vintage: serious, quality, top-of-its-game vintage that plays for our appetite for rosewood sideboards and vast, clean-lined seating. Not everything has a prestige designer attached to it – though Roberts manages to get his hands on a steady stream of pieces by Arne Vodder and Hans Wegner, among other Euro heavyweights – but those that don't will have lots in common with the popular midcentury schools, including excellent and innovative craftsmanship.

Two Columbia does have a sense of humour, though, and it comes out in the accessories: cocky plastic table lamps from the Atari era, for instance, and wood-burning stoves from swingin' 1960s chalets. You'll usually find these in the window, along with framed graphic art, some of it more ironic than others. And chances are it'll go for less than some retailers are charging in boutiques with higher rent. Recently a pair of vibrant *Acapulco* chairs was priced at 20 per cent less than two cousins less than a mile away. You know Roberts will have spotted that, too.

25 TWO COLUMBIA ROAD

- 2 COLUMBIA ROAD E2 7NN
- 020 7729 9933
- TWOCOLUMBIAROAD.CO.UK
- WED-FRI 12-7, SAT 12-6, SUN 10-3
- HOXTON

There's no mistaking the look of an Unto This Last product: the distinctive rounded corners, the stripe of the ply, sanded to an intangible grain, the origami folds and webbed-wood motifs. The craftsmanship is flawless, the output is all bespoke, and yet the prices are totally affordable to a Londoner's sensibility. There's an all-too-simple formula that makes this possible.

If you don't already know it, the John Ruskin's 1860 back-to-basics manifesto informed the esoteric name of the business. And for good reason. Unto This Last eschews the factory, warehouse and logistics of mass manufacturers by using high-tech equipment and uniform materials to produce bespoke interiors pieces expediently and, most vitally, cheaply. No packaging, no distribution and a minuscule supply chain mean the designers can do all their handiwork at this Brick Lane showroom-atelier – behind a wall of glass that gives it an almost 'while-u-wait' atmosphere (though lead times are realistically a couple of weeks).

Consequently, Unto This Last is like a testimonial for Ruskin's thesis: less dependence on industry and more on innovative technology for a minimal environmental footprint. It's a principle that surprisingly too few people are getting on board with.

26 UNTO THIS LAST

- 230 BRICK LANE E2 7EB
- 020 7613 0882
- UNTOTHISLAST.CO.UK
- DAILY 10-6
- SHOREDITCH HIGH STREET

27 YCN

📍 72 RIVINGTON STREET EC2A 3AY

📞 020 7033 2140

📍 YCNONLINE.COM

🕐 MON-FRI 10-6, SAT-SUN 11-4

🚇 SHOREDITCH HIGH STREET

The Young Creative Network has always aspired to do more than it says on the tin. Accordingly, it's got into the game of representing talent, then branched out to run its own creative agency. And several years ago it opened this gallery-shop to exhibit and sell the work of its more bankable members. Incidentally, membership to the YCN family is free, so it's debatable whether London's new creative talent is being discovered by YCN or the other way around.

Regardless, the talents displayed here are bona fide, from graphic artists like Andrew Clark, whose limited-edition giclée prints go for a kind £50 (£45 with a member's discount), to contemporary cartographer Herb Lester, whose city maps are propped up along one wall. The art extends to wrapping paper, scarves, greeting cards and postcards, like Fernando Volken Togni's neo-Deco *Geometrico* series.

The interior is a thing of beauty itself. Designed by London's Klassnik Corporation, its mobile vitrines and shelves fit back into the woodwork like pieces in a puzzle. The décor is as much a draw as the roster of art installations and the small but perfectly formed lending library in the back.

28 *French classics*

Stunning Conran-designed basement restaurant
and bar with glass-walled kitchen. Classic French
cooking, an impressive wine list & knowledgeable
staff make for a great dining experience.
BOUNDARY RESTAURANT & BAR
2-4 BOUNDARY STREET E2 7DD
020 7729 1051 | THEBOUNDARY.CO.UK

29 *All things pork*

From the founders of Terroirs in Covent Garden.
Informal, pared-back interior. Plenty of honest
dishes, including meaty and cheesy treats. Interest in
provenance. Exciting list of natural wines, too.
BRAWN 49 COLUMBIA ROAD E2 7RG
020 7729 5692 | BRAWN.CO

30 *Indian street food*

This second site of Dishoom is a near-perfect image
of the Irani cafés of Old Bombay. The indoor-
outdoor verandah is a colonial flashback. Affordable
menu of grilled street food and Chowpatty Beach
favourites.
DISHOOM [PICTURED] 7 BOUNDARY STREET E2 7JE
020 7420 9324 | DISHOOM.COM/SHOREDITCH

31 *Proper East End caff*

Tiny, family-run Art Deco café with local appeal.
Loved by city businessmen. Tasty, cheap, authentic
British/Italian meals. Full British breakfast is a must.
E PELLICCI 332 BETHNAL GREEN ROAD E2 0AG
020 7739 4873

32 *Cool dining*

'Coolest restaurant in London' from those behind
Upstairs at The Ten Bells. Five-course menu served
in the restaurant , snacks and mains served in the
bar alongside a precise cocktail list. Housed in the
Grade II-listed Shoreditch Town Hall.
THE CLOVE CLUB 380 OLD STREET EC1V 9LT
020 7729 6496 | THECLOVECLUB.COM

33 Michelin starred menus

Stunning French restaurant housed in old grand, red brick school from chef brothers Chris and Jeff Galvin. Superb cooking and garden dining for warmer months. Café A Vin next door offers more casual dining.

GALVIN LA CHAPELLE 35 SPITAL SQUARE E1 6DY
020 7299 0400 | GALVINRESTAURANTS.COM

34 European tavern

Restaurant and bar housed within a Victorian warehouse. Chef Angela Hartnett is in charge of a small seasonal menu inspired by Italian, French and Spanish cooking.

MERCHANTS TAVERN 35-42 CHARLOTTE ROAD EC2A 3PD
020 7060 5335 | MERCHANTSTAVERN.CO.UK

35 Coffee break

Coffee roaster and café from New Zealand with Antipodean menu on offer alongside their fine espresso blends and limited-edition daily roasted beans. A cavernous space with wooden beams, floor and central bar.

OZONE 11 LEONARD STREET EC2A 4AQ
020 7490 1039 | OZONECOFFEE.CO.UK

36 Hidden lunches

One of Shoreditch's best kept secrets. Canteen-style space in converted bike shed in the grounds of a former schoolhouse. Great home-cooked food. Buzzer entrance. Peaceful alfresco lunches in warmer weather.

ROCHELLE CANTEEN ROCHELLE SCHOOL, ARNOLD CIRCUS
E2 7ES |020 7729 5677 | ARNOLDANDHENDERSON.COM

37 Chicken, steak & art

Another successful Mark Hix restaurant, serving top-notch chicken and steak. The huge Grade II-listed tramshed now houses a specially commissioned artwork by Damien Hirst, *Cock and Bull* – preserved in a glass tank of formaldehyde, of course.

TRAMSHED 32 RIVINGTON STREET EC2A 3LX
020 7749 0478 | CHICKENANDSTEAK.CO.UK

Place to sleep? 38

ACE HOTEL LONDON SHOREDITCH ACEHOTEL.COM/LONDON

INTERNET SELLING *continued from p.141*

is that we can sell to parts of the country
where they don't have access to the kind
of products that we sell in London. Also,
on the internet, a customer can just make
a decision, order it and have it directly
delivered.

LINA KANAFANI

Yes, definitely, I am not denying that, it's just
how do we take advantage of it?

SHERIDAN COAKLEY

Don't you find that somebody in America could
just look on your website and see that
you have really interesting stuff and either
contact you via email or visit the next time
they're in London?

LINA KANAFANI

Absolutely, I think that most of our clients now
are from abroad, about 70% is international
and they have discovered us through our
website, then they email us. So that works
very well and without the internet this would
not have been possible.

MAX FRASER

Have you heard the term 'Showrooming'? This
is when people go into showrooms, then
use their smartphones to find the products
cheaper elsewhere. Do any of you have a
solution for this?

JUSTIN PRATT

It is human instinct to try this, and I hate the
idea of it, but I have done it. We've all done it
and therefore are all guilty.

SHERIDAN COAKLEY

I don't think that it happens that much. It's not
an epidemic in our business.

TRACEY NEULS

There is the mentality that because products
are discounted online, they can ask for it in
store. They are suddenly thinking that this is
the new marketplace.

MAGNUS ENGLUND

Unfortunately, I think that customers have a very
unrealistic view of the margins within
furniture. Customers might expect 25% off
without realising that it wipes out the profit.

SHERIDAN COAKLEY

I think that people should be allowed to sell
their products at whatever price they want to.
We have to step up as retailers to encourage

'SHOWROOMING'

people to come to our stores and do things
that online doesn't do.
NEIL SAUNDERS

Price integrity is important. We
have tended to see discounting from
big retailers that is like a drug and
they rely on it. I think that it is very
tempting to discount, but to me
discounting is almost an admission
that you have something wrong, unless
it is during a sale period. If you get
the product right, the service right and
the general mix right, you should be
able to keep that price integrity there.

This conversation was kindly hosted by Knoll
at their showroom in Clerkenwell (p.115)

de zeen watchstore

Watches by boutique brands and named designers

www.dezeenwatchstore.com

Southwark
& Bermondsey

SE1

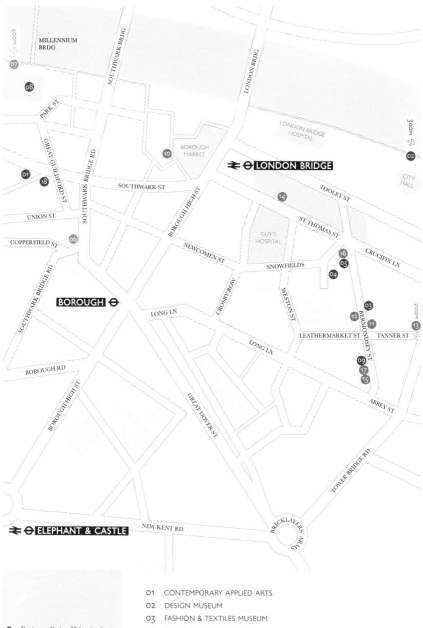

MILLENNIUM
BRDG

400M

07

08

PARK ST

GREAT GUILDFORD ST

SOUTHWARK BRDG

SOUTHWARK BRIDGE RD

01

18

UNION ST

COPPERFIELD ST

06

BOROUGH ⊖

SOUTHWARK BRIDGE RD

BOROUGH RD

BOROUGH HIGH ST

LONDON BRDG

BOROUGH
MARKET

10

SOUTHWARK ST

BOROUGH HIGH ST

NEWCOMEN ST

LONG LN

CROSBY ROW

LONG LN

GREAT DOVER ST

LONDON BRIDGE
HOSPITAL

300M

02

CITY
HALL

⇌ ⊖ LONDON BRIDGE

14

TOOLEY ST

ST THOMAS ST

GUY'S
HOSPITAL

SNOWFIELDS

WESTON ST

16
05

04

CRUCIFIX LN

03

12
11

BERMONDSEY ST

13

200M

LEATHERMARKET ST

TANNER ST

09
17
15

ABBEY ST

TOWER BRIDGE RD

⇌ ⊖ ELEPHANT & CASTLE   NEW KENT RD

BRICKLAYERS ARMS

- Design galleries & institutions
- Design shops & C20th vintage

- Eat & drink (pp.178-179)

01   CONTEMPORARY APPLIED ARTS
02   DESIGN MUSEUM
03   FASHION & TEXTILES MUSEUM
04   HELEN YARDLEY GALLERY
05   LONDON GLASSBLOWING
06   LOOPHOUSE
07   OXO TOWER WHARF
08   TATE MODERN
09   WHITE CUBE BERMONDSEY

Street*wise*

When did you move to this street?
We moved here in September 2009.

What originally attracted you to it?
The street was incredibly vibrant then, with a mix of exciting
places to eat, the Fashion and Textile Museum across the road,
the proximity of Borough Market – and we could see that, with
the building of The Shard and the upgrading of the London
Bridge area to come, this would be a great location for our
glassblowing studio and gallery.

**How has this shopping thoroughfare changed
since you've been here?**
The influx of wonderful new restaurants – Jose, Pizarro, Zucca
– and now Eames Fine Art has opened just two doors away from
us. Also, the finest contemporary art gallery White Cube has
opened on the street. This has made Bermondsey Street a major
London destination.

What does the street offer the community that is unique?
It has a great sense of community – a real village atmosphere
reminiscent of SoHo in New York. Great bars, eateries and
galleries form a social hub.

Tell us about some of your neighbouring hotspots.
Susie Stone is great little fashion business; Igloo has its main flower
shop here, and it also sells wine; the Fashion and Textile Museum
shows work from the greatest practitioners in the field; Holly & Lil's
dog boutique is possibly the best in London; the Vietnamese café,
with its outdoor seating in the park is an absolute gem; and I love all
the restaurants. For art, White Cube and Eames Fine Art are huge
assets in the mix.

If you could change one thing on the street, what would it be?
More galleries selling fine art would be excellent. We are now pretty
well served by restaurants, so galleries would make the street more
of an art destination.

Peter Layton
London Glassblowing

62-66 BERMONDSEY STREET SE1 3UD
020 7403 2800 LONDONGLASSBLOWING.CO.UK

BERMONDSEY STREET

01 CONTEMPORARY APPLIED ARTS

89 SOUTHWARK STREET SE1 0HX

020 7436 2344

CAA.ORG.UK

MON–SAT 10–6

SOUTHWARK

The petite storefront on Percy Street in Fitzrovia was sad to see CAA move on in 2013, but the modern treasures championed by this stalwart applied-arts gallery (pictured) warrant a new exhibition space with more heft. And the ground floor of this Grade II-listed former foundry, a quick shuffle from Tate Modern, is the place to do it. Modernised by Allies & Morrison, the RIBA award-winning practice located on the same block, the glorious vaulted interior has become a logical diversion from the Southbank gallery strip.

CAA has existed in some form or another since 1948, set up as a charity to sustain British makers through a new and more challenging era of crafting. These days, though, it's difficult to see whether the promotion was instrumental in moulding such high-calibre artisans or the other way around – they're that good. The organisation has hundreds of members, far too many to list here; suffice to say that many have gone on to successful careers, books and awards.

The gallery launches a new show every few months, curating among its members the finest glass, jewellery, fabrics and ceramics. The latter makes the shop particularly enriching. There's also a rich stock of books and periodicals, which are given greater emphasis at the new space.

In 2015, the Design Museum will move to West London to inhabit the former Commonwealth Institute, a midcentury pavilion undergoing an £80m redevelopment by architect John Pawson. Until then, however, the 25-year-old institution founded by Terence Conran will remain in its Art Deco digs at Shad Thames, gradually outgrown by the ambitious projects placed in the pipeline by director Deyan Sudjic.

The new launch will be the design event of 2015. Which isn't to say Shad Thames is living in limbo. There is always a reason to visit, if only to pick up a Royal VKB French carafe set in the shop or take tea in the café while watching the promenade on the Thames Path. The Designs of the Year exhibit, held each spring, highlights the key innovations to shape the world, saviours for developing countries and techno-revolutions for the modern existence, with one winner announced at the end of the run. The rest of the year you can trust Sudjic and his team to stay on top of the names you need to know, and the design projects transforming our world, with a rich programme of exhibitions and events.

⑫ DESIGN MUSEUM
- 📍 28 SHAD THAMES SE1 2YD
- 📞 020 7940 8790
- 🔗 DESIGNMUSEUM.ORG
- 🕐 DAILY 10-5:45
- Ⓔ LONDON BRIDGE

In siting her cutting-edge institution far behind the beaten Thames Path, fuchsia-haired designer Zandra Rhodes created a focal point for this fashionably offbeat community near Tower Bridge. The FTM's orange and fuchsia exterior was just the thing to liven up this strip of Bermondsey Street, too. Inside, a boldly painted colonnade leads into the exhibition rooms, where the giants of fashion are honoured with brave, well researched exhibitions. Textile designers like Lucienne Day, couturiers like Hardy Amies, and craftsmen like Kaffe Fassett have all been singled out for exhibits. The shop stocks a range of inventive jewellery and textiles, as well as a book selection that covers such contemporary conundrums as laser cutting textiles and designing repeat patterns on Photoshop.

⑬ FASHION & TEXTILE MUSEUM
- 📍 83 BERMONDSEY STREET SE1 3XF
- 📞 020 7407 8664
- 🔗 FTMLONDON.ORG
- 🕐 TUE-SAT 11-6
- Ⓔ LONDON BRIDGE/BOROUGH

The studio visit is not for everyone, but Helen Yardley makes you feel glad you came. The designer of hand-knotted and hand-tufted rugs has created a little patch of Yorkshire here in industrial Bermondsey. Up a Spartan stairwell, her samples are spread out like stepping stones, in colours that represent the English countryside (though my favourite is a wool and silk concoction called *Mars*). Most of her materials hail from Yorkshire and Dorset, though her New Zealand suppliers fill the gaps.

Yardley's techniques emanate from countries like Nepal and Iran with great rug-making traditions, but, she says, the hand-working is mostly done domestically these days, by artisans she knows and can rely on. The manufacturing line is kept busy with high-spec commissions from British architects furnishing large-scale projects around the world. But local residents visit for customised versions of the samples here, or attend clearance sales throughout the year. Her wall-hangings can also be viewed in exhibitions at Contemporary Applied Arts (p.172).

04 HELEN YARDLEY GALLERY

A–Z STUDIOS, 3-5 HARDWIDGE STREET SE1 3SY

020 7403 7114

HELENYARDLEY.COM

WED–FRI 11-5, OR BY APPOINTMENT

LONDON BRIDGE/BOROUGH

This old block of brown brick is exactly where you might imagine a glassblower would fire up his kilns. And yet, when you walk through the towering glass doors of artist Peter Layton's converted townhouse, sightlines all the way to the fiery furnaces in the workshop come as a shock. And a thrill. That's the point, of course. Layton, who launched the business back in 1976, when it was still one of the first 'hot glass studios' in Europe, wants to make his process as, erm, transparent as possible, so you can trace those *objets* on plinths back to the molten bubbles at the end of the blowpipe.

Layton offers a regular schedule of classes, but normally the workshop is run by his team of eight young resident artists, whose work you'll find in the front-end gallery. And in case you're wondering, these aren't your run-of-the-mill vases. The work of Layne Rowe possesses an otherworldliness with celestial swoops and alien pockmarks. Cathryn Shilling, on the other hand, shaves the glass paper thin and moulds it as if she's crumpled it up for the bin.

So if you are after a one-off piece of expertly crafted glass art to add an injection of colour and sculpture to your home, be sure to make a trip this way.

05 LONDON GLASSBLOWING

62-66 BERMONDSEY STREET SE1 3UD

020 7403 2800

LONDONGLASSBLOWING.CO.UK

MON–SAT 10-6

LONDON BRIDGE/BOROUGH

Now that most of us have ripped out the broadloom and refinished the hardwood, a robust new industry has taken over from the carpet warehouses of yore: rugmakers. More exciting and infinitely more creative than carpets, rugs can add another artistic element to a room, if you're so inclined. But as fun as they can be, finding the right one can also be debilitating. Lorraine Statham, who founded Loophouse more than two decades ago, will guide you with the understanding of an interior designer and the compassion of a mum.

Painterly pastels these are not: Statham prefers graphic, geometric patterns in saturated colours that you really have to see in situ to come to grips with. There are piles of books for that, and a website that features snaps from her corporate work with offices, restaurants and hotels across Europe and Asia. Because the standard sizes almost never make do in homes that are increasingly renovated beyond the standard floor plan, most customers opt for the bespoke service, rugs hand-tufted from 100% New Zealand wool.

Once you've sorted that out, you might turn your attention to the lines of wallpapers, cushions and beanbags. But do call ahead before you visit.

06 LOOPHOUSE
- 88 SOUTHWARK BRIDGE ROAD SE1 0EX
- 020 7207 7619
- LOOPHOUSE.COM
- MON-FRI 9.30-5.30
- BOROUGH

I'm always surprised when I find myself on a sunny Saturday browsing the shops at OXO entirely alone. Come sundown, people clamber to the top of the 1930s landmark for high-end cocktails and a view over the city, and yet many forget that some of the city's finest contemporary makers operate retail-ateliers on the floors below. A savvy conversion in the '90s by Coin Street Community Builders meant that creatives of wildly different persuasions could work on-site, attracting a market for their wares hot off the drafting table – or the loom, or the kiln. Most of those producers also do custom work.

You'll find the more successful collections delightfully recognisable. Bodo Sperlein, for instance, do ceramics for Mulberry and Lladró, among other homewares purveyors, along with its distinctive berry motifs. And Innermost's surreal light fixtures are regulars at design fairs worldwide. J-Me does handy desktop design; Miranda Watkins does flawless wood and metallic accessories; and there are literally dozens of start-ups who will sort you out with Christmas presents. That you can watch your gifts in the making is an added bonus.

07 OXO TOWER WHARF
- BARGEHOUSE STREET SE1 9PH
- 020 7021 1600
- COINSTREET.ORG
- TUE-SUN 11-6
- BLACKFRIARS/WATERLOO/SOUTHWARK

08 TATE MODERN

BANKSIDE SE1 9TG

020 7887 8888

TATE.ORG.UK/MODERN

SUN-THU 10-6, FRI-SAT 10-10

SOUTHWARK

You don't even have to cross the threshold to see why Tate Modern is the most visited modern art gallery in the world, with more than 4.7 million visitors annually. That location, for starters: looking back at Wren's St Paul's Cathedral over the once-wobbly Millennium Bridge with icons along the Thames for as far as the eye can see. And that great, yawning building: miles wide and graciously poised – you wonder why it took the city so many years to let it realise its potential.

But cross the threshold you should. One could go on for pages as to why the gallery is worth those five million bodies, the thematic displays of Rothkos and Matisses and Twomblys – indeed the permanent collection is blockbuster enough without the monthly headliners. But we're covering it for the superlative shop. In fact, there are four shops in all throughout the gallery, offering the requisite postcards and prints, but the space on the bottom floor belongs in some great museum shop hall of fame.

The wall of books alone, some rare, some signed, featuring artists from Alex Katz to Yayoi Kusama, in every genre of modern and contemporary, are displayed face out so you know what you're in for. The children's section is full of 'aha' moments, the jewellery is Tatty Devine-divine; the stationery delicious. Come early and come often: stock changes with the flavour of the exhibitions upstairs, but umpteen elbows will try to keep you from it.

09 WHITE CUBE BERMONDSEY

144-152 BERMONDSEY STREET SE1 3TQ

020 7930 5373

WHITECUBE.COM

TUE-SAT 10-6, SUN 12-6

BOROUGH

Lord knows how Jay Jopling, lord of the White Cubes, could ever top this 5,000-square-metre former warehouse, not only his largest gallery by far but the largest commercial gallery in Europe. In 2011, the sprawling 1970s brick space – more schoolhouse than art house – got a super-bright, super-contemporary, super-flexible makeover by Casper Mueller Kneer and opened during that year's Frieze Art Fair, when a world of patrons were on hand to pay their respects. And Jopling, whose stable includes Gormley, Gursky, Gilbert & George and the gamut of YBAS, was more than able to deliver.

There is obviously a lot to love here, particularly now that the White Cube in Hoxton Square has shuttered. But just as lovely is a wander around the cavernous bookshop with a takeaway coffee. You'll learn more in 30 minutes about the evolution of contemporary European art than in a month of classes.

10 *Market food*

Right in the heart of Borough Market is Elliot's, serving well-executed British food. All ingredients are from the traders in the market, and it's good. Exposed brickwork, glass-front with outside seating into the market. Open all day.

ELLIOT'S 12 STONEY STREET SE1 9AD
020 7403 7436 | ELLIOTSCAFE.COM

11 *Sunday roast*

Open for breakfast, lunch and dinner. Hugely popular pub serving good food alongside good beer/ale selection, cocktails and wine. There's a woodland cabin feel to the design, whitewashed walls, white tiles, mix-match of chairs and tables.

THE GARRISON 99-101 BERMONDSEY STREET SE1 3XB
020 7089 9355 | THEGARRISON.CO.UK

12 *Authentic tapas*

Corner site on Bermondsey Street, is often crowded, tricky to get a stall to perch at, but it's a must! Cava, wines and selection of sherries accompany daily changing small Spanish plates. Has a real Barcelona feel to it.

JOSE 104 BERMONDSEY STREET SE1 3UB
020 7403 4902 | JOSERESTAURANT.CO.UK

13 *Food indulgence*

This market has grown so much its serious competition to nearby touristy Borough Market. St John Bakery, veg supplier to chefs Natoora, Monmouth coffee, O'Shea's Butchery, and some brilliant small producers. Chance for cocktails and street food, too. Saturdays only.

MALTBY STREET SPA-TERMINUS.CO.UK

14 *Skyscraper dining*

Rainer Becker of Zuma fame opens his New York style restaurant in The Shard. Floor to ceiling windows offer best views of London as you tuck into a steak or lobster from the grill.

OBLIX AT THE SHARD LEVEL 32, THE SHARD, 31 ST THOMAS STREET SE1 9RY | 020 7268 6700 | OBLIXRESTAURANT.COM

● ● ●

15 *Spanish dining*

The godfather of Spanish cooking, Jose Pizarro, opened a second site on the same street. Red brick, booths, bar-dining, sharing tables, open kitchen and typical Spanish blue tiling. Stunning Spanish cooking, no reservations, open for lunch and dinner.

PIZARRO [PICTURED] 194 BERMONDSEY STREET SE1 3TQ
020 7378 9455 | PIZARRORESTAURANT.COM

● ● ●

16 *Nostalgic night out*

Newbie on Bermondsey Street, bar, restaurant and event space at the back. Russell Sage designed, interiors mimic an old-skool gymnasium. Ropes, climbing frames, those horses you had to jump over, all present & correct. Brilliant cocktails.

TANNER & CO 50 BERMONDSEY STREET SE1 3UD
020 7357 0244 | TANNERANDCO.CO.UK

● ● ● ● ● ●

17 *Italian lunch*

The white backdrop and simplicity of design allows Sam Harris' modern Italian food to shine. Ingredients are lovingly sourced and prepared, prices are good in this informal yet brilliant local Italian.

ZUCCA 183 BERMONDSEY STREET SE1 3TQ
020 7378 6809 | ZUCCALONDON.COM

Place to sleep? 18

CITIZEN M CITIZENM.COM

● ● ●

SAM JACOB

A city with no shops

* * *

"Shopping?" she said incredulously. "Here?" and she waved her arm down the High Street, at the bustling scene of public activity. "But why would anyone give all this up for… shopping?!" Then it struck me that she was way too young to remember how things used to be.

It's hard even for me to remember, partly because it seems so ridiculous, but town centres were once filled with people buying things, handing cards and cash over counters in exchange for stuff. People waddled down high streets with plastic bags stuffed with new things they barely needed. Shopping was what we did with our spare time, where we'd all go on a weekend to wander around in the presence of stuff. It was a collective hobby, a social event, a ritual through which we believed we were participating in public life, lubricated by gallon upon gallon of coffee.

Shops, I told her, were places where we went to conduct the secular worship of stuff. It was where we went to feel like good consumer-citizens. They were places we constructed our sense of self out of the things on offer. It was where we'd encounter new possibilities, new ways of being, new ideas, all in the form of products. This was what town centres had been given over to: the manufacture of personal identity through consumerism.

It's equally hard to remember the crisis, where whole high streets were boarded up. A combination of online retail, a tanking economy and the giant behemoths of out-of-town retail sucking away the life of the street. Plywood sheets went up over the big windows behind which goods had once been so provocatively arranged. The centres became deserted, except for a single garish 1980s-themed nightclub in every town that somehow, due perhaps to the eternal siren call of 1980s production techniques, evolved into a civic fixture over generations. The revival of the 1980s decade was, by now, well into its centenary.

At the time, the collapse of the high street seemed terrible. Everyone was convinced that retail was the foundation of community, the gravitational pull that kept us together as a society. Shopping had colonised public space so completely that we mistook it for democracy. And when it collapsed, it seemed like the end of something that had bound us together since the very earliest of human settlements.

It wasn't that everyone had stopped buying things. They were still there, clicking away with abandon, filling up their virtual carts, waiting by the door for parcels to be delivered. Ripping open brown cardboard boxes while they videoed themselves squealing about their 'hauls', posting their instant reactions to acquisition on internet sites. It wasn't that we cured ourselves of consumerism, it's just that we did it differently, in the privacy of our own homes, then overshared in the ultra-public of the internet.

The 'vacated middle', 'the donut': These were the strange names we gave the empty voids that had swallowed the places and spaces where we once had come together. The emptiness in the middle of our towns and cities became an existential crisis, as though urban form had replicated the hollowness we felt inside ourselves. The government even sent emissaries to these windswept pedestrianised deserts, often carrying cans of brightly coloured paint. These figures had bizarre titles like 'Queen of Shops'. It's where the word *Porticide* comes from:

Porticide [pôrt·i·sayhd] verb

Painting oneself into oblivion: *The centre of Barnsley committed total Porticide*

In other responses to the crisis, the brightest minds of a generation expended all their energy on things that flickered so very very brightly, then extinguished. *Pop-ups*, they called them: Bonfires of creativity, brilliant ideas scattered on the ash fields of the past, their intelligence and beauty doomed to fail.

But then something began to happen, one of those great flips from disaster to salvation that cities pull on us every generation or so driven by great bursts of energy that seem to emerge from nowhere. The same urban energy that had gentrified former slums, that had transformed industrial shells into artist studios and so on. Without warning the empty husks of retail began to flicker into life.

And like those other urban-flips, all it took was a mental reversal of polarity. It was all those other things, those things that really held us together that leaked back into the empty centres. Hospitals, which once had sat like autonomous islands within the cities they served, isolated by fences and seas of car parks. Schools that had once retreated from their boundaries in lonely paranoia. Universities opened lecture rooms, labs and studios that became places where cities and knowledge intersected. Pieces of government started to emerge in ways conversed directly with the public. Even rubbish dumps and recycling centres, once imagined as the lowest of the low, resited themselves right in the centre as vital social hubs. We started to go there not to consume things but to make things ourselves in the open access workshops and fab labs.

The idea of the high street had been totally transformed. It was no longer a place to buy stuff, but a place to engage, to learn, to really participate. It became host to the real mechanisms of society, not a place we went to buy the sensation of participation.

And shops? Well they did just fine, trading away from the margins of public life where they belonged. In time, Amazon converted the entire county of Warwickshire into a gigantic distribution warehouse from which all our needs could be delivered. Amazonville, the very real town sprouted on its roof, naturally has its own town centre. A town centre liberated from retail, free to act as the centre of public life.

* Sam Jacob is a director of architecture practice FAT

FASHIONARCHITECTURETASTE.COM

londondesignfestival.com

E9

N.8

Citywide

NW1

NW5

NW8

NW10

SE19

SW4

S.W.6

SW8

SW17

184

BRENT

CAMDEN

ISLINGTON

HACKNEY

KENSINGTON
& CHELSEA

WESTMINSTER

CITY

TOWER HAMLETS

HAMMERSMITH
& FULHAM

SOUTHWARK

WANDSWORTH

LAMBETH

LEWISHAM

MERTON

CROYDON

BROMLEY

- ● Design galleries & institutions
- ● Design shops & C20th vintage
- ● Design bookshops

Street*wise*

When did you move to this street?
In 1998.

What originally attracted you to it?
Apart from being a very central location, it felt very real at the
time. I was fed up with all the tourists in West London. I remember
walking home from the West End, crossing the old Hungerford
Bridge and there was hardly anyone walking along the South
Bank. It was a forgotten spot that was still affordable. Obviously
things are now very different.

How has the area changed since you've been here?
When I moved here, 'Cardboard City' [where the BFI IMAX cinema
is now] was still very much in evidence. There were bonfires every
night and I would often find a drunk homeless person sleeping
on my doorstep. Lower Marsh has always had an interesting mix
of shops. Very individual, run by eccentric owners. I'm glad it has
managed to maintain its character. The market in the street has
always been there but has changed in the type of things that
are sold. The clientele has also changed, as more people have
discovered this hidden spot.

What does the street offer the community that is unique?
There is an amazing sense of community around the area. It
feels like everyone knows each other, which allows for an
interesting mix of shop owners, market vendors, residents and
people that work in the neighbourhood. This does not really
exist in many places in London.

Tell us about some of your neighbouring hotspots.
Scooterworks (moped garage-turned-café), the Anchor and
Hope (gastropub), Gramex (secondhand bookshop run by
a retired architect and his wife), Radio Days (1950s vintage store),
Marie's Café (a cheap Thai restaurant serving great food) and
the Young Vic (theatre).

**What has recently changed on neighbouring roads
that has alarmed you?**
I've spotted Caffe Nero and Pret A Manger appearing on The Cut,
further down the road from us. This usually spells bad news, which
I hope won't spread.

If you could change one thing on the street, what would it be?
The multicoloured granite resurfacing that is about to be completed.
They used to shoot films here all the time, but I doubt this will still
be the case.

Michael Anastassiades
Michael Anastassiades Ltd   122 LOWER MARSH SE1 7AE
020 7928 7527 MICHAELANASTASSIADES.COM

LOWER MARSH

Footfall might not be the prime source of business of Lillie Road, but having trudged from West Brompton station past gigantic estates, a couple of pubs and an inexplicably gigantic health club, a charming stretch of road appears, crammed with antiques shops. Out of these, 52 Meters is by far the most exciting, eschewing the oxidised-zinc washtubs for theatrical Art Deco mirrors, 1950s Italian olive-wood side tables and school seats from Cambridge University that are more Prouvé than Prouvé.

The refreshing stock is the result of scouting trips by sure-eyed owners Henry Saywell and Tom Stewart-Liberty, who look out for Italian, French and Nordic lighting, in particular. One of their most interesting finds was a huge ceramic lipstick, part of the *Totem* collection, by Alessandro Mendini, and at the time of writing, a particularly good table light by Ettore Sottsass took pride of place in this worthwhile shop.

01 52 METERS
- 291 LILLIE ROAD SW6 7LL
- 020 7381 1774
- 52METERS.COM
- MON-SAT 10-5:30PM
- WEST BROMPTON

There are currently a dozen reasons for a vintage hound to visit Church Street, the Portobello Road of furniture. Each storefront is a window to a period in a past century, dripping with crystal, slathered in chrome, stashed with the vestiges of better times (rose-coloured glasses are the dealer's stock in trade). The pioneer on this otherwise folksy market street is Alfies, an old school warren of the sort more bankable neighbourhoods are criminally replacing with high-street chains.

Alfies has survived on the strength of its dealers – more than 75 in all, the highest concentration for miles. They're knowledgeable, well connected and beloved by magazine stylists across the country. They search far and wide to keep things interesting and refurbish to the highest standard (reupholstering with Kvadrat fabrics, no less), quoting you prices appended with that all-important 'ish'. You'll find ravishing period fashion here, hotel silver and cigarette ads from those 'better times', but what will really wow you are the midcentury antiques: Campo e Graffi side chairs, bronze lamps by Luciano Frigerio, steamer trunks, or a red-lacquer 1970s coffee table with a surface that reverses to black.

For Murano glass devotees, Alfies is the Holy Grail. Dealers like Thirteen, Francesca Martire and Vincenzo Caffarella stock over-the-top lighting festooned with fanciful glass shapes. And every piece has a pair.

03 ALFIES ANTIQUE MARKET
- 13-25 CHURCH STREET NW8 8DT
- 020 7723 6066
- ALFIESANTIQUES.COM
- TUE-SAT 10-6
- EDGWARE ROAD

Take a deep breath and enter this exhaustingly well stocked vintage emporium in the heart of Crystal Palace. Lights cover the ceiling and every available inch of wall groans with furniture and accessories, from sideboards and cocktail cabinets to lava lamps and colourful Swedish 1970s glassware. Owner Ains Phillips insists there are no reproductions or retro-style pieces here, just original pieces of the mostly-midcentury variety.

There are plans to reopen the basement and move the furniture downstairs. Meanwhile, once you're able to see the wood for the trees, it's not difficult to spot some lovely little gems here – a cool 1950s clock, Lucienne Day fabric and kitsch Babycham glasses, for example. There are some covetable large-scale pieces, too – I saw an original *Arco* lamp, some classic ceramic-topped 1960s coffee tables and a space-helmet-style Philips Discoverer TV.

With a background in engineering, Phillips has no problems restoring old electrical items – indeed, all lights, phones and clocks come with a one year warranty. When we visited, he'd just come back from sourcing industrial lights in Poland, which were being sandblasted and polished, ready for sale. He has as many ideas as his shop has stock, and his latest plans include more Art Deco pieces and a project with a local artist to make bespoke furniture from scrap metal.

05 BELLE COCO

- 40 CHURCH ROAD SE19 2ET
- 020 0011 1715
- BELLECOCO.COM
- THU, FRI & SUN 10-5, SAT 9-6
- CRYSTAL PALACE

The designer rules supreme in this Clapham Common showroom. As you enter, the names of the creatives behind the polished products take pride of place on a white wall, listing the likes of Shin Azumi, Marina Bautier, Robin Day, Matthew Hilton, Nazanin Kamali, William Warren and Samuel Wilkinson. Concentrating on delivering top-quality design en masse to retailers and clients, Case does an essential job in filling a gap in the market that too often gets high-jacked by mediocrity.

Here, there's no hint of the office-furniture showroom doldrums, where wood veneer and strip lighting feel like department store changing rooms – only solid craft, reliable lines and a pride in manufacturing skill so deftly personified in Matthew Hilton's products, as an example. Without a doubt, this place hits the mark for those looking for quality furniture that doesn't break the bank.

06 CASE FURNITURE

- 189 STONHOUSE STREET SW4 6BB
- 020 7622 3506
- CASEFURNITURE.CO.UK
- MON-FRI 10-6, SAT 10-4
- CLAPHAM COMMON

07 CHANNELS

🔻 1-3 NEW KING'S ROAD SW6 4SB

📞 020 7371 0301

↖ CHANNELSDESIGN.COM

🕐 MON-SAT 10-5:30

⊖ FULHAM BROADWAY

Noise from the Chelsea traffic outside recedes inside Channels, as does the rest of London's visual chaos. In here reigns a supreme calm, with an aesthetic peace emanating from Samuel Chan's furniture. There's wood everywhere, tactile and satin smooth, begging to be stroked.

Chan works in oak, walnut, reclaimed cedar, or whatever his bespoke clients want. There's a workshop in Shropshire and one in China producing clean-lined collections like the Finnieston – all sleek lines and sharp angles, but with a rougher, more organic floor lamp to break it up and create a glint-in-the-eye contrast. Overall, there's a Nordic/Asian vibe, with armchairs borrowing heavily from Wegner but adding scrolled armrests that wouldn't look out of place in the Forbidden City in the 1920s. Accessories are often Nordic, and always in pure materials (felt from Danish Inge Lindqvist, cast iron from Bengt & Lotta) that live happily together in this beautifully basic setting.

08 CHAPLINS

🔻 477-507 UXBRIDGE RD, HATCH END, MIDDX HA5 4JS

📞 020 8421 1779

↖ CHAPLINS.CO.UK

🕐 MON-SAT 10-6

⊖ HATCH END RAIL

Chaplins is most certainly the largest retailer of high-end furniture, lighting and interior products in London, or I should say Greater London, as this 2,500-square-metre showroom lies on the northwest fringes of the city. Driving here from the centre is a traffic-ridden nuisance – instead, take a train from Euston in 30 minutes and on the way you'll pass through a suburban swathe of the capital. Pop out at Hatch End and you've reached the wealth belt, where large houses prevail and they all need filling.

And that's where Chaplins steps in. Their enormous selection of top quality pieces is produced by a long list of manufacturers that reads like a who's who of leading European brands: Vitra, Moroso, B&B Italia, Moooi, Ligne Roset, Molteni & C, Cassina, Arper, Magis and many more. Items are given space to breathe in carefully styled room sets and staff are on hand to inform and advise. After all, buying anything at this level should be a considered investment (yes, some sofas really do sell for more than £10,000). Still, at least such decisions can be made sitting down.

09 ## CHASE & SORENSEN
238B DALSTON LANE E8 1LQ
020 8533 5523
CHASEANDSORENSEN.COM
MON-FRI 8-5, SAT 9-6, SUN 10-5
HACKNEY DOWNS RAIL

The demand for Danish modern furnishings is so vast and the market so savvy, there's very little of the stuff you could truly deem affordable any more. Dane Signe Sorensen and her partner Brent Chase are bringing prices back to earth with their flourishing East London business, thanks to a reliable network on the ground in Denmark that works full time sourcing slim-line teak and rosewood. These aren't flawless specimens from central banks and opera houses, rather pretty, homely, purposeful midcentury pieces that bring that familiar Scandi look just as effectively.

That is not to say there's no Wegner in store. You'll find it here and there, and without a middleman to pay off – the couple are able to price it within reach of even the Hackney locals. Upholstered rosewood armchairs by Finn Juhl and Arne Vodder's smoked-beechwood dining chairs make it to store fairly regularly. Still, this is a place happily free of label lust.

If you've never lived with Danish modern, visit the showroom-café on the fringes of Dalston, where you can settle into a 1960s sofa with a cappuccino and flip through the issue of *Bo Bedre* magazine sitting on the rosewood coffee table. Signe will zip back honest answers to all your questions, fill you in on their restoration business and brief you on what's on the floor at the new outlet in Victoria Park (110A Lauriston Road E9 7HA – open Fridays and weekends).

Located on a busy corner of Chamberlayne Road, this shop gives a confident first impression, with bold black and gold lettering and an enticing window display. Expect a nonchalant greeting from Alice the dog and a more genuine welcome from proprietor Mark Slade, who knows his stock inside out. The showroom is pretty packed, but the crowded nature of the space makes every item you see feel like a lucky discovery. The excitement of a junk shop without any junk.

Slade has an eye for well-designed pieces. Furniture and lighting, which date back as far as the 19th century right up to the mid-20th century, comes mostly from France and Italy. It's restored, rewired and reupholstered, resulting in a collection that ranges from pristine 1950s armchairs, to beautifully aged wood with a wonderful patina and rusty frames, complete with flaky paint. You may find some familiar names here – such as Franco Albini – but the vintage stock has been chosen for its visual appeal as much as its pedigree. Lighting is a particularly strong suit – everything from 1950s Italian chandeliers to colossal theatre lights – and there's always a good selection of mirrors and coffee tables, including plenty of brass.

10 CIRCUS ANTIQUES

- 60 CHAMBERLAYNE ROAD NW10 3JH
- 020 8968 8244
- CIRCUSANTIQUES.CO.UK
- TUE-SAT 10-6
- KENSAL GREEN/KENSAL RISE RAIL

It's a treat to find a purveyor of midcentury style who really knows their stuff, and Ben Adams, who's responsible for this fine collection, has the expertise to educate and inspire. You'll find him in the basement of a Victorian warehouse, tucked down the side of the estate agents' beloved Crystal Palace Triangle. Above him are floors filled with furniture from all sorts of eras, but in this patch it's all about handsome finds – often Danish or Dutch – dating from the 1950s to '70s.

You're likely to see some iconic pieces here, but the real treasures are less familiar – a sideboard by John and Sylvia Reid, a Fog & Mørup lamp or a poster from the Munich Olympics. If not obscure, then certainly in no danger of becoming ubiquitous. And if you're not sure what you're admiring, informative labelling will fill you in.

The furniture and lighting, sourced on regular trips to Holland, Antwerp and Stockholm, is of a consistently high quality. There's a particular bias towards combining metal and wood with lots of beautiful teak alongside some expertly reupholstered pieces such as an Ib Kofod-Larsen chair recovered in vintage tan leather and a Robin Day roll-back sofabed in Kvadrat fabric. A regularly updated website can keep you in the loop on the latest stock, but if you're able to visit in person, do. Browsing here is a delight.

11 DESIGNS OF MODERNITY

- CRYSTAL PALACE ANTIQUES, JASPER ROAD SE19 1SG
- 07966 285 694
- DESIGNSOFMODERNITY.COM
- MON-SAT 10-6, SUN 10-5
- CRYSTAL PALACE

12 DEZEEN WATCH STORE

100A STOKE NEWINGTON CHURCH STREET N16 0AP

020 7503 7319

DEZEENWATCHSTORE.COM

MON-FRI 9-5 OR BY APPOINTMENT

STOKE NEWINGTON RAIL

As the digital age ticks on and webzines evolve, we're seeing the men separate from the boys. In the realm of architecture and design, Dezeen has emerged as a daily must-read site, the source that even top design journalists consult before embarking on a story. The company has long since had a proper workspace, designed by Philippe Malouin of Hackney-based Post-Office, and for nearly as long it has operated an online shop for contemporary wristwatches. Recently, though, Dezeen called in Malouin again to create an exclusive boutique for the stock it keeps. The result is a spare plywood kiosk backed by industrial wire-grid shelving for high-concept pieces by designers such as Achille Castiglioni, Satoshi Wada and Nendo, as commissioned by Alessi, Issey Miyake, Hygge, and even Braun.

For now, the content is watches and watches only, but with Dezeen's growing clout on the design scene, we're waiting for more. For instance, on the back wall the office keeps a stash of Malouin's fold-up *Hanger Chairs*. The shop-minder says they're for staff use only; we hope they're a hint of what's to come.

13 DO SOUTH

2 WESTOW STREET SE19 3AH

020 8771 0500

DO-SOUTH.COM

THU-FRI 11-6, SAT 10-6, SUN 11-5

CRYSTAL PALACE

Occupying a prime corner spot with breathtaking views across London, this shop was established in 2011 with the aim of saving design-loving locals from having to trek into town. It was set up by Crystal Palace pair Noel Douglas and Freddie Oke, whose backgrounds in advertising and publishing gave them both a commercial and style-conscious approach. Their ability to select vintage and contemporary furniture is still evident, although these pieces have been joined by some questionable accessories of late. Nevertheless, Douglas's habit of simply buying chairs and tables that he likes is still a winning formula and his assertion that customers don't want either old or new pieces, but a bit of both, shows he knows his clientele.

The best bits of the contemporary collection are clean-lined yet comfortable sofas and there are some sleek sideboards, too, if you're not a fan of the midcentury variety. Vintage ornaments and homewares are a big pull, from a cluster of 1960s ceramics to a statement-making Mdina glass axehead vase. When it comes to the vintage furniture, names don't feature highly here, but who needs them when offerings include a nest of 1960s teak tables or a 1950s fluted-back chair, reupholstered in a cute pink fabric.

14 GEOFFREY DRAYTON
85 HAMPSTEAD ROAD NW1 2PL
020 7387 5840
GEOFFREY-DRAYTON.CO.UK
MON-SAT 10-6
WARREN STREET

North Londoners will likely have spotted this incongruous storefront from the window of a taxi or bus, an island of retail amid anonymous, windswept Euston Square. The wise among them have stopped for a look – Drayton is a legend in contemporary-design circles, after all, a 50-year veteran of the sort of European imports the younger generations must now take for granted.

The space, though enormous and entirely modern, wears its age on its sleeve, so to speak. It's packed to the rafters in the manner of the old-school dealers. If you're refurbishing, this is a smart jumping-off point, the reason being simply everything you could imagine is here in one place, the entire canon of furniture greats: Vitra, Magis, Knoll, B&B Italia, Interlübke, Flos, Cassina… If you have something specific in mind, one of the team will likely point to the very thing on the floor. If you're fuzzy on the particulars, he'll take you on a greatest-hits tour.

Try poking around on your own, too. Every piece is well marked with pedigree and price (sometimes, happily, cut to clear). I lost track of time testing chairs in the peaceful, catacomb-like basement. I might still be there if Drayton himself hadn't come down for a chat and whisked me back upstairs to marvel at a new delivery that he was excited to welcome into the fold.

16 HAUS

- 39 MORPETH ROAD E9 7LD
- 020 7536 9291
- HAUSLONDON.COM
- THU–SAT 11–6, SUN 11–5
- MILE END/BETHNAL GREEN

Victoria Park Village's Lauriston Road strip has been smartening up for a decade, but it really came of age when Haus signed the lease in 2009. A design shop with the heft of the central London purveyors but none of the attitude, Haus is run by Jane and Andrew Tye, who, with a strategic interior overhaul, have managed to show an impressive amount in their tight plot – of the sort of quality that puts a neighbourhood on the map.

A sculptor and designer respectively (Andrew produces his own designs through TYE3D), the couple are well versed in what will please and last. With that in mind, they support a balance of practical Scandinavians (Muuto, Hay, Massproductions) and Europeans (Vitra, Magis, Jasper Morrison) – with an occasional nod to green producers like Hampson Woods, who make chopping boards from trees felled in Russell Square. They also carry the *ne plus ultra* of pendant lighting. Hung cannily in groups of three are Tom Dixon's *Mirror Balls* and Foscarini's *Caboche*, though dozens of models lie in wait at the nearby warehouse to ship to online customers.

17 IKEA

- CROYDON, EDMONTON & WEMBLEY
- 0845 358 3364
- IKEA.COM/GB
- (SEE WEBSITE)
- (SEE WEBSITE)

People are always moaning about IKEA. It's miles from anywhere you'd want to be. It's maddeningly crowded. The queues are long. But I've always found that to be so much hyperbole, as if my managed expectations are destined to produce an experience more positive than expected.

The key to a successful IKEA experience is discipline. Plan ahead, go early and don't get distracted by the shelter-mag styling. If you follow the rules, you'll still leave with more than you came for, but not so much that you're a slave to your Allen key for days after. IKEA is ideal for the dining table you can't yet afford to commission, or the wardrobe that'll keep things off the floor in your new flat. The kitchenware is as good as any; ditto the kitchen cabinets and hardware. What you don't want is to 'over IKEA'. It's easy to do, but it'll make your home bland, cookie-cutter and, even worse, disposable.

As IKEA continues to expand into more cities, our awareness of the perils of disposable culture grows in tandem. How this will play out at IKEA HQ has yet to be determined. Will they buck the catalogue trend they started and go electronic? Will they use materials tough enough to stand the test of time? Or will their customers start voting with their feet?

18 INDISH

- 16 BROADWAY PARADE N8 9DE
- 020 8340 1188
- INDISH.CO.UK
- MON-SAT 10:30-5:30, SUN 12:30-4:30
- CROUCH HILL RAIL

The whole essence of this shop challenges locals to leave empty handed. The window lures them in with Iittala mugs, Kartell chairs and Ally Capellino bags and, safely within, time has a way of flying while they browse, some losing themselves for over an hour according to the shop assistant. There's a clear Nordic bent in the selection of stock, with names reading like a who's who of Scandinavian accessible design: Normann Copenhagen, Tonfisk, Design House Stockholm, Eva Solo, Marimekko and Stelton, with a substantial sprinkling of Alessi, Donna Wilson and Orla Kiely.

Lying in the shadow of the Crouch End clock tower, in one of the area's typical redbrick shop arcades, Indish has been an essential part of life in this genteel north London enclave for more than 15 years and provides an endless supply of Moomin mugs and colourful Kartell stools for style-eyed locals with some spare cash.

19 LASSCO

- 30 WANDSWORTH ROAD SW8 2LG
- 020 7394 2100
- LASSCO.CO.UK
- MON–FRI 9–5, SAT 10–5, SUN 11–5
- VAUXHALL

With traffic roaring past it, surrounded by hideously corporate architecture, Lassco, housed in a Georgian mansion, lies like an oasis of charm in the heart of Vauxhall. This is the place to come to buy salvaged Victorian pine altars, brass door knobs and plaster pilasters, but it's also an experience to savour – if it were a person, it would be the bewhiskered rear admiral who had had a tad too much port, speaking too loudly in a room full of accountants in Burton suits. And thank heaven for that.

Much more than an architectural salvage firm, Lassco's growing empire now stretches to a popular café at the Vauxhall site, outposts in Bermondsey and Oxfordshire, a reclaimed flooring business, and an events section that hosts everything from board meetings to ghost hunt – Vauxhall Pleasure Gardens may be gone, but this pocket of delight thankfully remains.

20 MICHAEL ANASTASSIADES

- 122 LOWER MARSH SE1 7AE
- 020 7928 7527
- MICHAELANASTASSIADES.COM
- BY APPOINTMENT ONLY
- WATERLOO

Gentrification might continue apace on the South Bank, but tucked behind Waterloo station lies Lower Marsh, an untouched slice of London at its most local best. Here shop owners live above their retail premises, and have done so for decades, while a street-food market feeds office workers on their lunch breaks. Designer Michael Anastassiades bought his studio-shop-living space here 15 years ago, back when crossing the Hungerford Bridge meant entering a land of cardboard cities and crumbling power stations. Since then, the area has changed as much as his house, which is now a carefully crafted living space with soaring glass walls and bespoke stairs and storage.

Downstairs is the gallery, with a display window facing the street, and a studio where Anastassiades and his team work on his own collection and recent collaborations with Svenskt Tenn and Flos, among other things. Staying independent and not thinking about work purely on a commercial basis is an important tenet of Anastassiades's production, and the symbiosis with his home is clear; his lights and mirrors were developed because he needed them in his house. The fact that other people also liked them, and wanted to buy them, turned out to be a bonus. At a visit here, guests have the opportunity to see design in real life, from the drawing board in the studio to the gallery – as real as the larger-than-life London street outside.

21 THE MODERN WAREHOUSE
- 3 TRAFALGAR MEWS E9 5JG
- 020 8986 0740
- THEMODERNWAREHOUSE.COM
- SAT 11-5, OR BY APPOINTMENT
- HACKNEY WICK

Why are you coming all the way out here? It's not to discover an obscure corner of Victoria Park, or even to rubberneck outside the Chapman brothers' studio across the lane. Nope: it's because you can't honestly call yourself a Scandinavian furniture buff until you've pored over the stock at Rob and David's warehouse. The partners – Rob works out of an office nearby, David at their Nottingham warehouse – got into importing back when it was a very lonely game. The market has since exploded, but MW's suppliers are steadfast and the logistics unchanged. Pieces plucked from airports, hotels and private homes travel by van to Nottingham, where they're repaired and reupholstered, if necessary, with Scandinavian fabrics true to the original ("We don't do anything funky," says Rob). A cross-section makes it to London for viewing, while the rest ships to online customers.

Hans Wegner fans will not go hungry here: he is the rule not the exception. There are also armies of leather-backed teak chairs by Finn Juhl, sculptural Ola Kettunen stools and two-tone armchairs by Ejner Larsen and Aksel Bender Madsen. Rob opens on Saturdays now, but he assures me he's thrilled to meet punters any time, provided they phone ahead.

23 PHILLIPS
- HOWICK PLACE SW1P 1BB
- 020 7318 4010
- PHILLIPS.COM
- MON-FRI 10-6 DURING EXHIBITION & VIEWING TIMES
- VICTORIA

This vast, white gallery space was once a postal sorting office and is now the London HQ of an internationally renowned auction house with a remarkable heritage. Founded in 1796, Phillips has held sales for Marie Antoinette and Napoleon Bonaparte and is the only business to have held an auction inside Buckingham Palace.

Auctions focus on the following themes: contemporary art, editions, photography, jewellery, and design. Lots can be viewed here in the week leading up to a sale with highlights on show at the Brook Street showroom. At other times, the Howick Place gallery holds selling exhibitions. Keep an eye on the website for details – they can be a great way to see celebrated work, such as Sebastiao Salgado's photography, without the crowds.

When it comes to design, there are two auctions held each year in London. The latest sale of 267 lots included exquisite 1950s chairs by Gio Ponti, Poul Henningsen lighting dating from the 1930s, and furniture by Poul Kjaerholm and Hans Wegner. This generous space is the perfect backdrop to show off the lots and accommodate the eager bidders. If you can't be there, get a slice of the excitement by following it on Twitter.

Just as Indish mirrors the tastes and buying patterns of Crouch End's design cognoscenti (p.194), Placesandspaces caters for Clapham's Stokke-toting mums and dads. There's a clear predilection for wooden toys in the shop, with games from Brio and Kay Bojesen's monkey swinging from the shelves, but also Asplund sideboards and Jieldé floor lamps for the grown-ups' delectation. The Scandinavians are heavily represented, with the now ubiquitous Moomin cups lovingly displayed and Form Us With Love's industrial lamp for Design House Stockholm shedding a gentle light on the tasteful, grey walls. But it's Charlene Mullen's embroidered cityscapes that best substantiate this cultivated part of Clapham – urban, but with a quirky, elevated touch.

Outside, it's a shame about the through traffic, as otherwise the triangular Old Town would be the ideal spilling-onto-the-pavement drinking spot, surrounded as it is by cafés and no less than three pubs.

24 PLACESANDSPACES
- 30 OLD TOWN SW4 0LB
- 020 7498 0998
- PLACESANDSPACES.COM
- TUE-SAT 10-5:45, SUN 12-4
- CLAPHAM COMMON

One of the only reasons to visit Camden's Stables Market these days, Planet Bazaar is mercifully cosseted among Moroccan importers, some distance from Goth Central. Though it may, nevertheless, take you an hour to track it down, it shouldn't be long before you find something you want to take home. Even those weary of polyurethane *Egg* chairs and 1960s ceramics will be able to see past the clutter.

Maureen Silverman has been trading in mementos from the 1950s through to the '80s since the latter decade had barely passed. She's still in store daily and will pop out from behind a stack of metal garden chairs to offer background or arrange a delivery. Silverman clearly loves the stuff she stocks and will teach you to love it too, if you're not so inclined. Recently she pointed out a darling tulip-based breakfast table, whose yellow leaves prop up to form a flower-shaped surface, and enumerated the charms of a 1960s teak sewing table whose surface slid back to reveal a storage space.

This is no jumble sale: prices are affordable yet not rock bottom (it's fodder for the Primrose Hill set, after all). There are always gems, however: Italian modern table lamps, a surfeit of Jacobsen and Eames, and all the Chippy Heath telephone tables a flat can accommodate.

25 PLANET BAZAAR
- STABLES MARKET, CHALK FARM ROAD NW1 8AH
- 020 7485 6000
- PLANETBAZAAR.CO.UK
- TUE-FRI 12-5, SAT-SUN 10-5.30
- CHALK FARM

26 PRIMROSE HILL INTERIORS
☞ 115 REGENT'S PARK ROAD NW1 8UR
✆ 020 7722 6622
↖ ESSENTIALVINTAGE.COM
🕐 TUE–SAT 11–6, SUN 12–5
⊖ CHALK FARM

If the citizens of Primrose Hill like their décor classic with a hint of offbeat, Primrose Hill Interiors has sniffed out the ideal locale for its showroom, a well-heeled, pulled-together salon with a bit of edge leftover from a former life in Camden (that's the business and, very likely, the clientele). Owner Phil Cowan carries the requisite midcentury Danish and Dutch wood, cabinets, coffee tables and credenzas in rosewood and teak. But he mixes it up with Art Deco from Italy and German storage from the 1970s, some pieces inset with unusually artful panelling and washed with silver leaf (even upholstered chairs), making you feel as if you're trespassing on someone's elegant boudoir.

Cowan has a way with lighting and deals overwhelming in Italian pieces from the 1960s and '70s. His Murano-glass pendants are like hanging sculpture, adorned with unusual cloudy details and in colours you can't quite place. Banana milk? Tobacco yellow? They nonetheless shine against the white leather sofas that make occasional appearances. Framed landscape paintings on the walls don't quite have the same polish, but you're not here for the art, are you.

27 RETROUVIUS
☞ 1016 HARROW ROAD NW10 5NS
✆ 020 8960 6060
↖ RETROUVIUS.COM
🕐 MON–SAT 10–6
⊖ KENSAL GREEN

The beauty of this salvage shop (and it is beautiful) lies in its simplicity and repetitiveness. Set on the soulless Harrow Road, just up the road from Kensal Green station, visitors who use the old door pull are admitted to the mother lode of architectural features and near-antique products. Stacks of scuffed, white lampshades take on a new soul due to their piled-up positioning against dark tongue-and-groove panelling, while rugs, artlessly flung over a banister, gain an added layer of appeal purely due to their plenitude.

Directors Adam Hills and Maria Speake have chiseled a whole new aesthetic out of found objects, a style magazines sometimes call 'rough luxe', 'British eclectic' or even the dreaded 'shabby chic'. But seeing all the products in situ, working together with the cavernous warehouse, they take on a whole new lease of life, breathing beauty in a way they probably never did fresh from the production line and workshop. It's a design style much emulated, but rarely bettered.

28 ROCA LONDON GALLERY

STATION COURT, TOWNMEAD ROAD SW6 2PY
020 7610 9503
ROCALONDONGALLERY.COM
MON-FRI 9-5:30, SAT 11-5
IMPERIAL WHARF

In 2011, a remarkable space landed in the most unsuspecting of London addresses. I say 'landed' because this is the most striking and futuristic bathroom showroom you are ever likely to find, designed by the great dame of pioneering architecture Zaha Hadid.

Roca, one of the world's leading producers of bathroom products, boldly commissioned this flagship space to communicate its products and brand vision in an altogether more dynamic environment. In her signature style, Hadid translated the powerful movement of water into the sculpted forms of the white concrete space, giving it the appearance that it's been eroded and polished by fluidity.

At a base level, this is a 1,100-square-metre showroom for the Spanish brand to display its taps, basins, toilets and baths. Beyond that, it also hosts an array of exhibitions and talks that draw attention to the global importance of water for humanity, offering enterprising solutions to water shortage, pollution and distribution.

29 ROCKET

4-6 SHEEP LANE E8 4QS
020 7729 7594
ROCKETGALLERY.COM
CHECK WEBSITE
BETHNAL GREEN/LONDON FIELDS RAIL

Collectors and fans of Dutch, Danish and American modernist furniture and bold geometric art should already be familiar with Rocket, having enjoyed many years of its exhibitions and displays at its Shoreditch gallery. In the latter half of 2013, owner Jonathan Stephenson moved the gallery to a new space behind Broadway Market, doubling in size.

Spread over two levels, complete with outdoor terrace, the premises are divided into spaces for art, furniture and two-dimensional design and play host to exhibitions four times a year. Rocket has more recently become a mecca for Dutch design from the 1950s and '60s with collectible items by the likes of Martin Visser, Wim Rietveld and their contemporaries, complemented by a specialist archive and sales website (dutchmodernism.com).

Stephenson isn't afraid to mix design and art. He's furnished an exhibit of Michelle Grabner's 'Flapjack' paintings with reissued pieces by Danish modernist Jens Risom. And he's supplemented a show of Keld Helmer-Petersen's monochrome photographs with books featuring his earlier colour oeuvre.

Books are another of Stephenson's passions and a honed selection is for sale here. Onsite is a design studio for typography and book design, where art and design catalogues and artists' books are published under The Rocket Press imprint. Whatever your favoured genre, the content throughout Rocket is of the finest order.

SOUTHBANK CENTRE SHOP

- FESTIVAL TERRACE SE1 8XX
- 020 7921 0771
- MON-FRI 10-9, SAT 10-8, SUN 12-8
- SOUTHBANKCENTRE.CO.UK
- WATERLOO

Between the southern exit of the Golden Jubilee footbridge and the Royal Festival Hall lies the expertly curated Southbank Centre Shop. Filled with colourful gadgets, idiosyncratic prints and vanguard design, visitors here feel as select as the crowd attending one of the events in the cultural grounds surrounding it, with the Hayward Gallery, BFI, Royal Festival Hall, Queen Elizabeth Hall and National Theatre crowding around in all their concrete splendour.

Whether it's a conscious effort or not by buyer Katherine Walsh, the shop mirrors the ethos of inclusiveness that was the basis of the Festival of Britain back in 1951, making design and art accessible to all without conceding on quality and vision. In the choice of products there are also discernible threads backwards, with Mini Modern's wallpaper harking back to a midcentury aesthetic, but this is weighed up by an equally strong forward vision, as can be seen in the *Flux* chairs, made from one foldable sheet of polypropylene.

Every three months a fresh batch of products come courtesy of the designer-makers of Cockpit Arts, creating a great platform to catch the eye of design-savvy buyers – the best-selling item here at the moment might be the Ryan Gosling colouring-in book, but Paul Catherall's London prints come a close second, showing the successful width of this design outlet.

31 THE WAPPING PROJECT

WAPPING WALL E1W 3SG
020 7680 2080
THEWAPPINGPROJECT.COM
MON–SAT 12–10.30, SUN 12–5.30
WAPPING

Unless you live in East London, you really need a reason to trek to Wapping, an industrial-age relic of a neighbourhood. The Wapping Project is this reason for hordes of design-minded Londoners with a sense of adventure. Theatre director Jules Wright put Wapping on the map when, in 2000, she converted this defunct hydraulic power station into a one-stop shop for eating, meeting and art-gazing, scattering the voluminous space with slick black tables and a rotating roster of designer chairs. Since that time the 'hood has come up, with young professionals colonising the ubiquitous converted warehouses and using the Project as their hub.

There's no best time to visit this vast brick pile, set behind iron gates and still furnished with the original mechanics and heavy iron hooks. On weekend mornings the place echoes with the buzz of brunchers downing bellinis and feasting on elaborate eggs and homemade breads before heading over the road to the Thamesfront beach. You can enjoy an elegant lunch of grilled fish and Australian wine, then linger in the greenhouse bookshop. Or pass an evening over a lively dinner and, between courses, descend to the gallery housed in the former filter house. Wright attracts artists budding and established, who experiment with the vaulted space and earn accolades from the critics.

WELLCOME COLLECTION

32

183 EUSTON ROAD NW1 2BE

020 7611 2222

WELLCOMECOLLECTION.ORG

TUE-SAT 10-6, THU 10-10, SUN 11-6

EUSTON SQUARE/EUSTON

When the Design Museum (p.173) stages its annual Designs of the Year exhibition, some of the most highly anticipated innovations – if the least sexy – are those that promote health and well being. Where the Wellcome Collection differs is that it makes even medicine sexy. Located in a 1932 neoclassical pile, a rare treasure beyond the fug of Euston Road, it houses a library, event halls, gift shop and accommodating Peyton & Byrne café, but most exciting are its collections of medical curiosities (from Japanese sex toys to Napoleon's toothbrush) and its schedule of out-there exhibits, which highlight the confluence of life, death, discovery, progress, art and design.

Run from a trust set up by the late Sir Henry Solomon Wellcome, the organisation has made brilliant work of its mandate. Last year, the airy ground-floor space hosted an enticing (and rather grotesque) exhibition of iconography related to death. And later it curated a collection of outsider art, called Souzou, from Japan. A series of bright spaces upstairs hosts the permanent collection, wired with nifty technology that encourages interaction. Skeletons are curiously jumbled; a transparent body has organs that light up when you push their buttons; supersized minibeasts appear in vitrines. It's especially suited to kids, but the real beauty is in the wonder it stirs from the grown-ups. Oh, and it's free.

oca London Gallery by Zaha Hadid Architects

The inspiration that flows from water.

Station Court, Townmead Road, London, SW6 2PY, UK
Phone: + 44 (0) 20 7610 9503 • info.londongallery@roca.net

Opening times:
Mondays to Fridays from 9am to 5:30pm
Saturdays from 11am to 5pm

www.rocalondongallery.com
f – Follow us

Roca
THE LEADING GLOBAL
BATHROOM BRAND
www.roca.com

LONDON
DESIGN GUIDE
.com

Register to receive monthly news updates,
promotions and special reader benefits
throughout the year.

British Library Cataloguing-in-Publication data. A catalogue
record for this book is available from the British Library.

The research for this publication was completed in 2013.
Although the authors, editors, and publisher made every effort
to ensure that the information contained in this publication is
up-to-date and as accurate as possible at the time of going to
press, some details are liable to change. The publisher accepts
no responsibility for any loss, injury, or inconvenience sustained
to any person using this book.

Printed in China by Everbest Printing Co. Ltd

Publisher's acknowledgements: Spotlight Press would like to
thank all contributing shops, galleries, institutions, designers,
manufacturers, agencies and photographers for their kind
permissions to reproduce their images in this book.

The editor would like to dedicate this book to his wife, Hannah.

Trade orders: Central Books, orders@centralbooks.com
centralbooks.com. For further distribution details and
advertising enquiries, visit: londondesignguide.com

ISBN: 978-0-9563098-3-9

Photography credits: all images credited to and courtesy of
the titled businesses unless stated otherwise. We apologise in
advance for any unintentional omissions and would be pleased
to insert the appropriate credit in any subsequent publication.

(13) Eric Laignel (17) bottom Inge Clemente (19) Jonathan Root
(21) © 2007 John Offenbach (24) Luke Hayes (40) top © Peer
Lindgreen (41) bottom Pelle Crepin(53) Paul Raeside (55) top
Marimekko Corporation (57) Andrew Meredith (59) top Khalid
Bazzi (63) Mark Weeks (68) top Richard Church (70) pieces by
Mattia Bonetti (74-75) Mark Weeks (81) top Agnese Sanvito;
bottom Mark Weeks (82) Sanna Fisher-Payne (83) Installation
view of 'M/M (Paris) The Carpetalogue' at Gallery Libby Sellers,
2012. Photography by Ed Reeve (85) Jake Curtis (90-91) Mark
Weeks (96) Paul Raeside (97) Mark Weeks (98) Peer Lindgreen
(103) © Jeff Knowles (106-107) Mark Weeks (112) Andy Stagg (113)
courtesy of the Barbican Centre (115) top Marco Fazio; bottom
Grant Smith (116) bottom Mark Whitfield Photography (119) top
Jan Baldwin; bottom Mark Whitfield Photography (121) Luke
Hayes (124-125) Mark Weeks (133) bottom Aida Nedzelskyte
(134) bottom Ed Reeve (135) bottom Rupert J Tapper (140-141)
Mark Weeks (146) bottom Ross S. Fury (147) bottom Suzie
Winsor (148) Petr Krejci/courtesy of Gallery FUMI (149) Geffrye
Museum/Richard Davies (150) Nicola Tree (152) A. Moran/Labour
and Wait (155) bottom Paul Raeside (160) top Sandra Lane;
bottom Yu Fujiwara (161) top Annie Smith anniephotosmith.com
(163) Spencer Wilton for YCN (166-167) Mark Weeks (172) Allies
and Morrison (173) top Luke Hayes; bottom Mark Weeks (177)
Gilbert & George 'London Pictures', White Cube: Mason's Yard,
Bermondsey, Hoxton 9 March - 12 May 2012 © Gilbert & George.
Photo: Prudence Cuming Associates Ltd/Courtesy White Cube
(188) bottom Frankie Ruffolo (191) top Luke Hayes; bottom James
Balston (194) top Inter IKEA System P.V. 1999-2011 (197) bottom
Dan Reaney (200) Paul Tucker/courtesy Rocket (202) Wellcome
Library, London.

⊖ © ® Transport for London
Underground Roundel logo reproduced by kind permission of
Transport for London

Index

442577

Notes